RECRUITMENT AND SELECTION

Gareth Roberts is a consultant in human resource management and has assisted many organisations in the development of competency frameworks, and related approaches to pay, performance, and selection. Prior to his consulting role, he worked in senior human resource roles with Lloyds Bank, Warner-Lambert Confectionery, Parke-Davis Pharmaceuticals, and the Health Service. He lectures at the Civil Service College and is a member of the Industrial Tribunals. He is on the IPD's register of consultants.

Other titles in the series:

The Institute of Personnel and Development is the leading publisher of books and reports for personnel and training professionals, students, and for all those concerned with the effective management and development of people at work. For details of all our titles, please contact the Publishing Department:
tel. 0208-263 3387
fax 0208-263 3850
e-mail publish@ipd.co.uk
The catalogue of all IPD titles can be viewed on the IPD website:
www.ipd.co.uk

RECRUITMENT AND SELECTION

Gareth Roberts

INSTITUTE OF PERSONNEL AND DEVELOPMENT

For Denise
— the best selection decision I ever made

First published in 1997

Reprinted 1999

Design by Paperweight
Typeset by The Comp-Room, Aylesbury
Printed in Great Britain by
The Cromwell Press, Wiltshire

IBM RC
18 95

British Library Cataloguing in Publication Data
A catalogue record for this book is available from the
British Library

ISBN 0-85292-707-X

The views expressed in this book are the author's own, and
may not necessarily reflect those of the IPD.

iD

**INSTITUTE OF PERSONNEL
AND DEVELOPMENT**

IPD House, Camp Road, London SW19 4UX
Tel: 0208 971 9000   Fax: 0208 263 3333
Registered office as above. Registered Charity No. 1038333
A company limited by guarantee. Registered in England No. 2931892

CONTENTS

PREFACE

This book is intended as a practical guide to the process of recruitment and selection. It aims to provide an analysis of the key aspects of all elements of the selection process, which will be of interest to students of the subject, but its main purpose is to provide practical advice and guidance to those involved, at whatever level, in the recruitment and selection of people.

ACKNOWLEDGEMENTS

It was over 20 years ago when I first read Philip Plumbley's book on recruitment and selection. I was up to my neck in recruitment activity as a young personnel officer and very grateful for any advice; I could not have wished for better than that book. It has been a source of wisdom I have called upon many times since, and it remains one of the few management books I can truly say I have enjoyed reading. I was delighted, but apprehensive, at being asked to write its successor. I hope that I have succeeded in following the hard act of producing a text which combines practical guidance for those involved in recruitment, with sufficient coverage of the issues for those interested in its study. I have sought to reflect the changes which have taken place in recent years, in academic research, the changing role of work, opportunities from technology, best practice, and the ever-changing law (stated as at June 1997).

I am grateful to many people for their help and advice in the preparation of this book but particular mention must go to some. Russell Drakeley of CGR has been a great source of advice on biodata as well as being a patient martyr to the lost cause of trying to make me understand statistical correlation, selection ratio, and all the other heavy stuff. Adrian Furnham, Professor of Psychology at University College, London has helped me greatly on psychological testing, as well as making me understand the importance of an open mind. David Rayner has been the legal eagle, to whom I am indebted for keeping me up to speed on legislative changes and case law. Denise Roberts has worked wonders on turning around the manuscript.

Thanks must go to Bob Whitney of MSL, Richard Mycroft of UK Passport Agency, David Lawrence of The Coastguard Agency, John Tarrant of TMP Advertising, Allan Cameron of

CIM Test Publishers, and to ASE Test Publishers, for the opportunity to share their material. Thanks also to Matthew Reisz and his team at IPD for help and encouragement.

PART 1

CONTEXT

1

THE SELECTION PROCESS

The purpose of selection is to match people to work. It is the most important element in any organisation's management of people simply because it is not possible to optimise the effectiveness of human resources, by whatever method, if there is a less than adequate match.

Well-designed organisations cannot excel by the quality of design alone – neither praise nor pay can motivate people to perform beyond their capabilities, and the best training programme cannot make a silk purse from a sow's ear. Without the basic match of people and work, it will not be possible to gain a proper return on all the other investment in human resource programmes. 'Work' is more than the range of tasks and activities undertaken; it includes the physical, economic, and social environment in which the activities take place.

In the twentieth century, selection has been primarily concerned with matching people to specific jobs. In the twenty-first century the importance of flexibility and the rapid pace of change make it more important to look at matching work in the wider context. It becomes necessary, in assessing people, to look beyond the skills for the specific job in hand, and to look at the potential range of matches for the person, be it future work, mobility in and out of the organisation, interaction with a wide range of potential colleagues, and fit with the current and 'social' environment of customers, suppliers, culture etc, and the 'physical' environment, particularly technology.

Mintzberg has said that strategy is the stream in which a range of disparate activities takes place. In that vein, selection is often strategic; a range of activities is undertaken in the general 'stream' of finding people to 'fill a role'. Effective selection is more akin to a total quality approach, in which measurement is a vital tool, the specification is clear and all activities carefully orchestrated to play a specific part in a grand design in which the whole is greater that the sum of the parts.

The key elements in selection are:

- a clear and precise specification
- effective use of multiple techniques
- elimination of redundant processes
- measurement
- evaluation and continuous improvement.

Figure 1 shows the stages in a typical selection process.

Person specification

The process begins with a very clear specification. Selection is like searching for the proverbial needle in a haystack. Good selection techniques may remove the hay effectively, but being able to clearly recognise the needle is essential.

The specification embraces a profile of the role and of the ideal person to fill that role. Since selection is about matching people to roles, it is important that both sides of the equation are clearly specified. Poor selectors overlook the necessity of clear role information. Good selectors understand that one of the best judges of a candidate's suitability for a role is the candidate; helping candidates to gain a clear assessment of the role will provide important benefits. Careful scrutiny of the role provides, of course, other 'hidden' benefits beyond pure selection. It enables decisions to be made on whether the role is necessary, whether it should be redesigned or reviewed, whether its 'pecking order' and reward status in the organisation are correct, whether it should be a training role for others, and a host of other HR management issues not purely related to selection. Since most employment tends to be for a significant duration, it is important to look to the future and consider planned and potential changes to the role.

Figure 1
SELECTION PROCESS FLOW-CHART

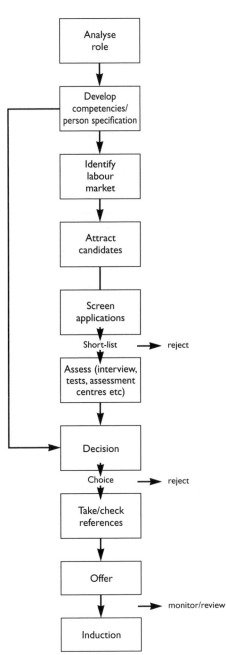

Competencies

One of the key aspects of determining the role and person specifications is the use of competencies. The use and development of competencies are described in Chapter 5. The term 'competencies' is used to describe all the work-related personal attributes, knowledge, experience, skills and values that a person draws on to perform their work well. In many HR applications, such as training or performance management, the competencies are described in terms of behaviours and patterns of work, and the focus is on those competencies which differentiate between effective and superior performance. For selection purposes a slightly broader approach needs to be taken, for a number of reasons.

First, it is not appropriate to focus only on the competencies which differentiate superior from effective performance. In selection there needs to be a great concern with all the competencies which underpin effective performance because the selection process will be the threshold to separate the unsuitable from the suitable. None of the 'basic' competencies can therefore be ignored.

Second, providing descriptions of the competencies in terms of everyday work behaviours is of only limited value. It is highly likely that candidates will be external to the organisation, and/or in a different area of work. There may therefore be no 'track record' of the behaviours. Where the candidate is coming from a similar role, this usually means from another organisation and it will be difficult to get hold of evidence of the competencies.

Third, there are great practical constraints which may render it difficult to get examples of the candidates displaying the competencies in everyday work behaviour. This may be because the candidate has no directly comparable work experience or because it is not possible to seek the opinions of those currently able to observe, particularly if they are in another organisation.

Finally, and perhaps most importantly, seeing the behaviours in the current setting does not necessarily mean they will be repeated in the new role. It may be a reflection of the environment, the organisation style or the way the person is managed, and which may or may not transfer easily to a different

environment, culture, or role. It is important, therefore, to consider the competencies which will provide evidence of potential performance as much as those that give evidence of a
'track record'.

The use of competencies extends beyond simply 'measuring' the candidate. It is important to match the candidate and
the role. The candidate can play an important role in self-
assessment of suitability. Competency-based role descriptions
help candidates to get a feel for the role in a way that 'logical'
job information and traditional job descriptions do not. The
incorporation of values and standards helps to ensure that the
hearts as well as the minds of potential candidates are
attracted to the role.

Attracting

The initial part of the selection process is concerned with
'selling' the role. Considerable thought needs to be given to
this part of the process, particularly where external advertising is being used. Very few organisations would countenance
their products being marketed in 'one-off' disparate uncoordi-
nated advertisements. The expenditure on selection advertising rarely achieves the same heights as product advertising,
but it is not loose change. A single newspaper advertisement
can represent a significant proportion of a starting salary. The
expenditure on advertising therefore needs to be carefully targeted and form a part of the overall marketing strategy for
employment. This means a co-ordinated on-going campaign
in which key messages are communicated cost-effectively
through appropriate media. In developing an employment
marketing strategy, a similar process to that for developing a
product strategy needs to be followed. Setting the values, the
selling proposition, the target audience, and the communication channels are essential components. This aspect is considered further in Chapter 8.

The process of attracting people to apply for the role
requires achievement of a balance. There need to be sufficient
candidates to afford an opportunity to choose, but the quality
of candidates needs to be good enough to make such decisions
meaningful. There is a much greater sense of satisfaction for

line managers in making a difficult choice from a high-quality pool of similar candidates than there is in selecting the candidate who stands head and shoulders above his or her fellow candidates. There is also a very important cost consideration in the processing of unsuitable applications. Some organisations, notably some 'professional' selection consultants, choose to reduce costs by declining to acknowledge the application and/or keep the candidate informed of progress. This is a false economy and carries the disadvantage of creating a poor image of the organisation. The correct approach is to pro-actively manage the response rate through the provision of useful information, and related techniques, to assist in self-selection.

The information on the organisation and role will be useful, but more is not necessarily better; there is an optimum. Research, for example, on candidates' use of glossy company brochures shows that little of the information is used to guide the candidate's decision to apply; it is most frequently used to help the candidate prepare for interview. The most useful ways of providing information are to give candidates a preview of the work undertaken or to provide a job information questionnaire. Job previews are very useful but are logistically difficult to organise in large volume recruitment; although open evenings, temporary postings, and work experience have been run effectively in a range of organisations. The job information questionnaire is a method by which information is 'drip-fed' in response to a range of questions about the role, which the candidate completes and self-scores. Advice related to the level of score can discourage potentially unsuitable applicants from proceeding further with their application. This has dual benefits in avoiding administration costs and not having to reject candidates. Candidates who have 'rejected' themselves are less likely to be hostile to the company. For many organisations there is always a risk rejected candidates become lost customers.

Response

The response process is usually based on application forms or curricula vitae. The use of application forms adds an additional stage to the overall selection process because the initial contact from the candidate has to be followed with a response in sending out the forms. There is, however, the opportunity to send the other information described above and, on occasions, it may therefore be ultimately more cost effective than dealing with direct applications. The use of an application form means a standardised response against which a great number of candidates can be assessed. Care needs to be taken in designing a form so that necessary information can be gleaned from it. This may seem an obvious point but the form serves a dual purpose; it is a mechanism for screening but it is also a reference source for addresses, references etc. There is sometimes a tendency for the reference-source needs to push out the screening-information needs. The form should concentrate on a small number of key competencies capable of being assessed from the form. There is a temptation to try to extract too much information from the form. Motives, values and personality characteristics cannot be gleaned from an application form; they are better identified through testing and interviewing. The form, and its screening process, need to focus on the acquired knowledge, skills, experience pertinent to the role.

It is usually most effective to incorporate monitoring forms with the initial response. The forms ought to be separate from the application form so that they are seen to be separate from selection decisions. They will be used to monitor compliance to legal requirements on race, sex and disability discrimination as well as quality standards. This is further discussed in Chapter 4.

Screening

The application-screening process has attracted little research attention, but a research project undertaken by Herriot and Wingrove in 1984 revealed that the process is generally subjective, inconsistent and lacking focus. Providing selectors with a clear idea of the competencies to focus on when screening the application form, together with examples of good or poor evidence, will significantly improve the quality and consistency of the selection process. A similar principle can be applied to the screening of curricula vitae, although the varied nature of each candidate's CV makes the task more difficult and time-consuming.

Variations on the screening process occur in a number of ways. In tele-sales and other telephone-based services, it is customary to undertake the initial screening over the telephone. The advertisement will provide a telephone number, with set call-times, and the candidate's call is answered by a screening person, using a defined script (for consistency) and scoring method for rating answers. Candidates are not rejected (because of the adverse reaction) but 'streamed', with the fast stream proceeding quickly to the next stage.

A variation on the application form is the use of biodata (biographical data). This is a technique that dates from the 1920s but, despite high levels of predictive validity, does not enjoy common usage. It is easiest to describe as a set of questions framed around 'coincidences' in the lives of people who are good performers. The concept is widely used in the financial services industry for approval of loans, insurance, etc. People are generally accustomed to the concept in car insurance – the model of car driven and postcode area of address will dictate the level of insurance premium payable. It is, however, much less common in selection, and carries some degree of sensitivity. For selection purposes it would be necessary to ask a group of employees to provide information about themselves through answering a wide-ranging questionnaire, then looking for correlations in the answers that seem to differentiate between high- and low-performers. The reasons for the differences may not be known or understood, but their occurrence will provide the basis on which to screen applications.

Following the initial screening process, the use of selection methods varies more widely between organisations and between the kinds of recruitment. Some organisations will use interviews, some will use psychometric tests, some will use work simulation or role plays and some will use an assessment centre comprising a range of techniques.

Interviewing

Interviewing is the most frequently-used selection technique; it is very unusual for people to be hired without an interview. Interviews may be either structured or unstructured. The unstructured interview generally takes the form of a free-ranging discussion, sometimes with the interviewer using a set of 'favourite' questions but providing the interviewee with a free rein to answer in a general way. In an unstructured interview, the interviewer uses his or her judgement about the overall performance of the candidate in deciding whether he or she matches the role.

The unstructured interview is the most commonly-used interview; it is frequently used by professional selectors from search and selection agencies who have confidence in their ability to assess candidates without the constraints of a structured interview.

Research suggests that the unstructured interview is half as effective as a structured interview. The structured interview is focused on a set number of clearly defined criteria, usually competencies. The questions are carefully structured to obtain specific information about the criteria and the answers are scored against a consistent scoring range. In situational interviewing candidates are presented with a future hypothetical situation and asked to explain how they would deal with it. The answers are assessed for evidence of relevant ability. Recent research shows that the behavioural and experience interviews are a more effective form of structured interview. In the behavioural and experience interview, the questions are aimed at drawing out past examples of behaviours, linked to specific competencies. The interviewer compares the answers to positive and negative descriptions of the behaviours, scores each of the competencies and makes a judgement based on the scores.

Although interviewing is one of the best-established selection techniques, it suffers from a number of problems. It is difficult for the interviewer to sustain attention throughout the interview, with interviewers sometimes able to remember only the opening and closing stages of the interview. Judgement of interviews can sometimes be clouded by prejudices or influenced unduly by stereotyping the candidate with, for example, others in his or her organisation, or by 'mirroring', in which the interviewer looks more favourably on candidates matching the interviewer's own profile. Perhaps the most common failing of interviews is the lack of preparation on the part of the interviewer.

Regardless of its problems the interview remains one of the most popular selection techniques; whatever its 'technical' value in the selection process, it is of great perceived value to selectors and a very important aspect for candidates.

Testing

Psychometric tests have gained significantly in popularity in recent years, but are by no means commonplace. Tests can either be of ability or personality. Ability tests measure specific aptitudes such as, for example, vocabulary, numeracy, spatial awareness, typing speed and accuracy. They are used most commonly in selection for clerical positions. Ability tests are generally more accurate in predicting potential than are personality tests. The most frequent cause of legal claims arising from test use is with ability tests, often because selectors use the test without considering whether the ability it measures is essential for the job. For example, testing train drivers for vocabulary may discriminate against those whose native tongue is not English, and may bear no relation to potential ability to drive trains.

Personality tests are used to measure the range of personal characteristics, values and attitudes which shape an individual's beliefs and behaviours. There are various theories of personality, but most psychologists agree on a basic five-factor model, known as the 'big five', the permutations of which will form the many varieties of 'personality'. Most proprietary personality tests measure one or all of the five factors, albeit that some tests may subdivide into a larger number of dimensions. There is dispute over whether or not personality tests can predict job performance, with plentiful evidence to back both views. In the UK there are constraints imposed by The British Psychological Society on the use of tests, so that personality tests may be used only by a psychologist or someone trained to BPS Level B. The constraints are imposed because the interpretation and feedback of test results requires expertise.

Ability tests are tests in the true sense of the word, since they measure in an absolute sense the degree of aptitude required. The higher the score on the ability test, the better that person will be (in that ability). Ability tests usually *feel* like tests, have exam-type questions and strict time limits for completion. Personality tests are not tests as such; there are no elements of pass or fail. Each aspect of personality is a continuum with good and bad features at both extremes. The measures on a personality test are benchmarks (known as norms) with others in the group so it is important to know which aspects are causally related to a job performance, and have benchmark information (normative data) on job holders in order to judge the results. Personality tests do not usually look like tests but are often a series of questions or adjectives with which the candidate simply agrees or disagrees. In addition to 'omnibus' tests measuring the full range of personality, there are specific tests measuring single dimensions or specific values or particular attitudes. There are about 100,000 psychometric tests available world wide.

Exercises

There are no foolproof selection techniques – there is nothing that comes close to 100 per cent accuracy in predicting future job performance. The only way to be certain that someone can do the job is to give them the job; technically sound, perhaps, but fraught with practical difficulties and cost implications. The next best thing may therefore be to give candidates a preview of the role and provide some work simulations on which to base a judgement of their performance. Such role plays and simulations are frequently to be found in assessment centres, although there are occasions when they are used alone.

The key elements in establishing work simulations are to develop exercises which are realistic, are capable of being observed and evaluated, which encourage true rather than artificial behaviours from candidates, and are cost effective. Developing realistic exercises means measuring those aspects which are causally related to job performance. One of the

criticisms of work simulations is that they tend to seek ide-
alised responses which are based on assumed good behaviours
rather than being anchored in any empirically based
researched examples. It is sometimes said that candidates in
a work simulation are assessed against the designer's idea of
how the work should be done rather than the way job holders
work in real life.

The nature of exercises varies. Sometimes they take the
form of individual work. For example, a candidate may be
given an in-tray of sample mail and asked to prioritise and
respond in order to assess prioritisation, work organisation
and understanding. Sometimes the exercises are abstract
assignments designed around teamwork so that the interpersonal skills of candidates can be observed. In observed exercises the judgement of observers is highly important and
necessitates clear instructions and training.

The limited use of exercises and work simulations is a
reflection mainly of costs. There are some off-the-shelf exercises but they may require customising; most exercises need
to be designed from scratch. There are also significant
resource costs involved in providing (and training) sufficient
observers. There is also a discomfort factor in candidates
'playing games', which tends to target such exercises on
school leaver and graduate recruitment. There are, however,
some novel adaptations. The use of 'trial by sausage roll' is
popular in selection of salespeople or public profile roles, and
usually takes the form of an informal buffet reception for candidates but during which a number of 'hosts' are required to
assess the candidates on the way they 'work the floor' and
identify, and build relationships with, key influencers at the
reception. In high-cost or high-risk occupations the use of
simulations, eg flight simulators for pilots, can be a very cost-
effective and safe means of assessing potential.

Assessment centres

Assessment centres involve the application of a number of
techniques over a prolonged period in order to build a comprehensive picture of the candidate. A typical assessment
centre will last at least one day, and often a number of days. It

will usually comprise some visits and presentations of information on the organisation, one or more structured interviews, testing, work simulations and exercises, and perhaps some element of 'trial by sausage role'. Assessors are brought together for debriefing and provide their evaluation of candidates based on overall performance through all the assessment elements. Assessment centres are most often used in graduate recruitment, partly because the investment in graduate trainees is usually high, and partly because candidates already in employment find it difficult to commit to a long assessment process.

Assessment centres have the highest predictive validity of all the selection techniques but they are an amalgam of techniques rather than a technique in their own right. It is important, in developing cost-effective assessment centres, to ensure that the candidate specification is clear, that the different techniques are matched most effectively to particular criteria, and that there is an effective evaluation process for bringing the results of the various techniques into an overall assessment.

Checks and offers

The information on candidates needs to be checked for authenticity. This may include documentary checks on qualifications, licences, etc, statutory checks on work eligibility, specialist checks on health and credit or criminal records, and taking up references. The use of references is one of the most universal aspects of selection even though there is unease when giving them, and cynicism when receiving them. There are legal obligations, in providing references, to the recipient and the subject. References are generally more useful when the request is framed around specific questions.

Offers of employment may be conditional or unconditional. Conditional offers are sometimes based on pre-conditions such as receipt of satisfactory references or achievement of an academic qualification. Some offers are post-conditional, for example they may be subject to satisfactory completion of probationary period. Offers need to be clear and explicit, and although there are no legal requirements for a written contract of employment, there is a legal requirement for a statement of main terms and conditions to be provided within two months of taking up employment. Offering different terms to people based on gender, race, or disability is unlawful discrimination even if the person turns down the offer.

Follow-up

Recruitment and selection is often viewed as the process up to the decision on the candidate. The information gained on the candidate is often placed with the recruitment file and retained in case of any discrimination claims or other complaints. The information gathered is, however, of great potential value in managing the person. It is often the case that the final selection is a compromise, that no candidate perfectly matches the specification, and that an offer is made to the person who most closely matches the specification. It is important, therefore, to plan the induction process to meet the needs of that person, to review the role design to see whether it requires changing (the new person may need more or less supervision than envisaged, for example), and to provide his or her new manager with information on the way in which they can be managed for best results. The more structured the selection process, the easier it will be to identify these key elements. In competency-based selection there is the added advantage of being able to track development, manage on-going performance, and link pay to competencies so that selection becomes the start of a process rather than the end.

As well as concentrating on ensuring the candidate adjusts to the new role, it is important to review the process itself. Using utility analysis techniques, described in Chapter 16, it is possible to calculate the cost-effectiveness of the selection process but some key data need to be collected to support this. Organisations find it useful to track costs and measures along each stage of the process. At the advertising stage, the response rate to each form of publicity needs to be monitored, not only in absolute terms but also showing proportions of respondents going on to the different stages and to final selection. The correlation of interview, test and exercise success to application form and CV information needs to be analysed, to identify future targets. The cost of each stage and technique needs to be clearly identified (including internal labour costs) both in gross terms and as a ratio to successful candidates. The effectiveness of the different stages and techniques needs to be assessed; this is best done by reference to the subsequent evaluation of the candidate's work performance to see whether the techniques accurately predicted the outcome. Where different techniques provide the same clues, it needs to be questioned whether both are needed or whether reliance could safely be placed on one.

In addition to information on the cost and effectiveness of the process, there needs to be monitoring of the standards. These include both quality and legal aspects. Quality will be reflected in the speed of response – whether all applications were acknowledged, etc, and may include service questionnaires for clients (including internal) and candidates (successful and unsuccessful). The legal aspects will need to include monitoring of response rates and success rates for ethnic minorities, male v female, and disabled. Age discrimination, although not unlawful in the UK, may still feature in the monitoring. Care should be taken to monitor the effect of mechanistic processes such as tests and biodata in creating indirect discrimination.

2

LABOUR MARKETS

Types of market

Since recruitment and selection is about buying labour into the organisation it is important to consider the markets in which such 'purchases' are undertaken .

Economic

The classic economic theories divide labour markets into internal and external markets and into primary and secondary markets.

The internal labour market is classically defined as the market within a single organisation, as opposed to the general labour market covering all forms of employment. In traditional terms this was an effective way of describing the classical approach to employment in which employees took on life-long careers with an organisation and remained in employment with that organisation whether in the same role or, more usually, through a series of hierarchical promotion opportunities. The external market was concerned with all those who were either in employment or available for employment and it is this group that is featured in all statistical information on labour markets, whether produced by government bodies or others.

The significant restructuring of employment patterns in the 1980s and 1990s has caused a significant shift so that the internal market is now sometimes more loosely defined as those employed within a given sector or industry. Thus the internal market for chemists may once have been defined as the organisation in which they were employed, eg ICI, but nowadays may be defined as the chemical industry generally.

Social

Sociological terms to describe labour markets have been primary and secondary labour markets. The primary market relates to those in full-time long-term employment. The secondary market relates to those in casual, part-time, or temporary work. There have, however, been sociological changes which impact on this perspective. The UK approach to developing the competitiveness of companies through organisational restructuring has been fundamentally different from that adopted in other parts of Europe. The emphasis in France and Germany in particular has been the retraining and redevelopment of people in order to change workplace or occupational work group. In the UK the 'investment' has been deflected from retraining and into 'buying-off' resistance through enhanced severance packages. This has been a trend largely dominated by government initiatives in industries such as steel, coal and transport. The effect has been to create the new phenomenon of primary, secondary and tertiary markets. Primary labour markets are those in which individuals enjoy a demand for their labour and benefit from virtually continuous, stable (though not necessarily free of insecurity) and economically worthwhile employment. The secondary market is categorised by those in casual, part-time or temporary positions and where individuals may need to change jobs frequently, perhaps hopping between permanent, interim and temporary positions, and where the emphasis is on securing immediate financial solvency rather than long-term career planning. The tertiary labour market is characterised by a residual group of people without immediate or long-term prospects of 'normal' employment, either operating in the black economy or reliant upon welfare, charity, crime or other forms of income generation. The nature of the secondary market has been particularly impacted by the approaches to redundancy used by organisations in the 1980s and 1990s. In particular, the so called 'lemon' effect has operated in which the bad drive out the good as a result of uncertainty about the quality of people needed. Studies by outplacement consultants such as Coutts and others have shown that redundancy leavers generally have higher levels of intelligence, relevant experience, risk-taking, creativity and other qualities than the redundancy survivors. The structuring of severance packages generally favours those of higher age or longer experience, who may not necessarily be those most able to re-enter the labour market. The effect of these two phenomena is that it discourages the leavers from re-entering the primary labour market and puts them into the secondary labour market where they may either choose to pursue self-employment rather than salaried employment or to 'down-shift' in lifestyle with the subsidy of an early pension.

Geographic

A third way of looking at labour markets is on a geographical basis. Traditionally we have been concerned with the difference between local and national markets since some labour is constrained for economic or other reasons to the locality, while 'career' jobs have tended to operate on a national market. Thus, lower-paid manual or clerical positions would tend to be resourced from the local labour markets while professional, technical or managerial roles are more likely to be resourced from the national labour market. This view of the labour market has also changed significantly in recent decades. The advent of the single European market brought with it, as part of the Treaty of Rome, the requirement for mobility of labour across the single market. Although there is no clear evidence of European-wide policies on HR management being deployed by organisations, and no clear evidence of Eurocentric human resource policies, there is a noticeable shift towards a European dimension in resourcing in organisations in the UK and there are key influences such as joint venture organisations (for example Airbus Industrie) and acquired industries (for example BMW's acquisition of Rover, and French acquisitions of utility companies) which have played a significant part in creating a pan-European market in some technical and managerial areas. While the single market may have encouraged the free movement of labour, the movement of capital is now on a truly global basis and it is now the case that 'jobs' can flow more easily around the world than 'labour'. The see-sawing of jobs between Europe and the Far

East has been evidence of this trend, but perhaps of greater significance in the long term is the impact of global technology. Airline tickets, insurance policies and other intangible goods ordered over the telephone or through a computer network may be processed in an entirely different country from the one in which the order originated.

Labour market changes

As outlined above, there have been significant organisational, social and economic changes that have caused us to view labour markets in different ways. In the UK labour market (in its widest sense) there have been some very noticeable trends which impact upon recruitment activity.

- Labour shortages in the 1980s which accompanied growth of organisations have turned to a labour surplus following universal trends to downsizing. This has generally meant a reduction in the workforce but has rarely been accompanied by real improvements in productivity and therefore there has been no additional wealth creation to provide redeployment opportunities for the displaced. Political manipulation of unemployment figures masks the true extent of out-of-work people, but it is clear that that there is a labour surplus which, though slowly declining, will prevail for some time.

- Skills shortages prevail in spite of labour surplus and government intervention (such as Training and Enterprise Councils and National Vocational Qualifications) and such skills shortages are deteriorating in each reported year.

- The age composition of the labour market is changing in line with demographic changes so that there are fewer young people and a greater number of older people in the population generally.

- The gender composition of the employment market is changing so that male employment is declining and any growth in employment is in female employment.

- There is a sectoral shift from manufacturing industry, in which employment is steadily declining, to the leisure and retail sectors where there is growth in employment.

Accessing markets

There are different methods by which employers 'fish in the pool' of labour. Such methods include:

- employment centres, such as careers service or job centres or unemployment offices
- agencies, sometimes for temporary positions, sometimes for permanent positions and sometimes as an out-sourced operation in which the agency acts as a provider of services rather than a broker for labour
- consultants to undertake search and selection, particularly when searching for high-level or more specialised positions where there may be a need to tap into an industry market
- advertising through various media, whether on a local, national or international basis and whether on a general or specialised focus.

The fundamental changes to labour markets and to organisations in recent decades necessitate a rethink of the approach to the market. In the 1960s Chris Argyris spoke of the legal and psychological contracts which govern the employment relationship. This is a useful model on which to draw. The traditional view of labour markets as economic, social or geographic models may need to be replaced by a psychological model. So, too, must the demand-side of the equation be reconsidered. Organisations are moving more frequently to a model of core and peripheral workforces and, within the core workforce, looking at career and non-career positions. Consumer marketing has moved from simplistic economic segmentation to the use of psychographics. Originally developed by the Bureau of Applied Research in the USA in the 1930s, psychographics evolved from the proposition that any research aimed at understanding consumer behaviour must 'involve an interplay among the three broad sets of variables: predisposition, influences and product attributes'. In Chapter 8, the application of consumer product marketing techniques to the marketing of employment is discussed, and the parallel therefore needs to be drawn at this stage between understanding consumer psychology in relation to product purchase and understanding a labour market psychology in relation to employment-seeking. It has been observed that, in consumer product marketing, psychographic research is used to:

- identify target markets
- provide better explanations of consumer behaviour
- improve a company's strategic marketing efforts
- minimise risks for new products and business ventures.

The first three will have valuable parallels in achieving efficiencies in recruitment advertising or other approaches to the labour market, but the fourth principle is the one of significant interest for recruitment, in as much as the major concern for recruiters is to improve the probability of selecting suitable employees and minimising the risks of poor placement. The march of psychographics will not have escaped many people; readers of this book may have recent experience of being asked to complete a form, whether from a supermarket 'special offer' promotion or on the purchase of a new consumer product with the warranty registration, or from the subscriptions department of a magazine, etc, seeking a host of information on hobbies, preferences for types of television programmes, income and many other facets which extend beyond simply the economic or lifestyle classifications.

Countered against the psychological view is the proposition that people are rational, that they pursue employment for wholly economic terms. Interestingly, most studies of labour turnover indicate that economic considerations (ie leaving for a better-paid job) form a minority, about 3 per cent, of the reasons to leave. Reasons for joining are rarely, if ever, researched by organisations but there is some research evidence about candidates' reactions to the way they were treated during the selection process, which suggests that emotional considerations can often be as significant as rational ones. It is also interesting, from the opposite viewpoint, that a study of the selection of young people by small businesses (employing about one-third of the total UK workforce) showed that recruiters regarded the 'emotive' aspects of personality and interest as more important than the 'rational' aspects of ability, aptitude or attainment. The same study also showed that the main approaches to the labour market were through:

- career service, used by 36 per cent
- employment service or unemployment benefit office, used by 25 per cent
- advertising, used by 24 per cent
- local training provider, used by 23 per cent
- asking current employees, used by 18 per cent
- asking friends and associates, used by 13 per cent
- maintaining lists of unsolicited applications, used by 14 per cent.

It is, of course, not as simple as looking only at the psychological or emotive aspects, regarding the approach to the labour market as some kind of dating agency, matching common interests and outlooks. Recruitment of engineers, for example, needs to be undertaken from a pool of engineers and the recruitment of solicitors needs to be undertaken from the pool of legally qualified people (disregarding apprenticeship and articles for the purpose of this illustration), and the consideration of personality and other issues would therefore be a subsidiary concern. There are, however, many employment opportunities which are not so constrained by considerations of qualification and, indeed, it is often the case that flexibility to adapt to changing roles and circumstances is a prime requirement. In such circumstances consideration of the psychographic labour market, rather than traditional approaches, will be of great practical value. One of the current limitations is that the budget of a marketing department is far greater than that of a human resources department and it is unlikely that many organisations would be able to conduct their own psychographic research. It is also the case that readily available psychographic research, such as YCS and SRI International, are consumer rather than employment based. There are, however, many organisations where product market research could be used; supermarkets are, for example, a growth area in employment and at the forefront of psychographic research, often through the medium of their loyalty cards and, coupled with an induction audit of new employees, would provide an extremely useful tool for targeting recruitment activity and expenditure.

Whichever model of the labour market is chosen, it is important to bear that market in mind when deciding on the approach to it. Attempting to tap into the market for chemical engineers, for example, may not be successful through the use of employment centres if there is low unemployment among chemical engineers; nor will local advertising yield results unless there is a high concentration of chemical industry in the locality. It is likely to be more effective to tap into the employment of chemical engineers by regarding them as a national, European or global market and advertising in a trade journal, or by using selection consultants specialising in the industry. Giving thought to the market to be tapped will therefore help in developing a cost-effective approach to recruitment from that market.

Care needs to be taken at this stage to avoid discrimination. It has been said, for example, that advertising in certain prestige newspapers or journals will be hidden from under-privileged groups; that using newer technology such as the internet may discriminate against older groups, that cinema advertising may discriminate against the blind; and radio advertising against the deaf; and that some media will discriminate against ethnic groups. The labels used here may not be politically correct but they may help to reinforce the point that care needs to be taken not to perpetuate discrimination indirectly through unconscious use of an approach because of custom or habit.

3

SELECTION AND HR STRATEGY

There is an old saying that 'you can't make a silk purse of a sow's ear'. This holds true in the context of an organisation's human resources strategy, since without the right people in place the human resources strategy will be expending effort on making good the shortfall rather than capitalising on the asset and leveraging for optimum organisation performance. One of the frequent calls of business leaders today is the need to change the organisation's culture which, on closer examination, often means trying to get people to do the things they should be doing in the first place, in the way in which they should be doing them. It may not be over-simplistic to say that it would be more effective to have employed the people who are capable of doing the work being done, who were predisposed to doing it in the way the organisation would wish to see it done, and who were conditioned from the beginning of the employment relationship into such commitment. Significant amounts of money and effort are expended, in countless organisations, on organisational design strategies to ameliorate the problems of mis-placed people, on redundancy programmes to rid the organisation of people who should never have been selected, or of jobs which should never have been filled. Similarly, in some organisations precious training resources are squandered in trying to train round pegs to fit square holes. It is also the case that pay policies are sometimes made to sweat too hard in order to condition patterns of behaviour which the organisation should really be able to take for granted. These are, of course, bold statements and they have no universal truth, but neither are they universally irrelevant; the point is that many organisations can enjoy improvements to business performance by improving recruitment and selection practices.

In recent years selection in the UK has been the focus of much improvement as organisations recognise the pivotal role it plays in the overall human resources strategy. It is pivotal, however, in more than simply the sense that the quality of the people will determine the quality of the organisation. There is the role that recruitment plays in shaping people's expectations and conditioning their attitudes and contribution on entry, and in gathering a rich source of information on people's skills, values, motives etc, which can play an essential part in providing the intelligence upon which other human resource policies can be shaped. The links between the selection practices and other human resource policies need to be made explicit.

Specifications

One of the most important parts of the selection process has for long been the development of a clear specification upon which the selection activity is based. Good selectors have always followed this discipline rather than 'shooting in the dark'. It has, however, been a fairly transient phase; once the successful candidate has been appointed, the specification has been disregarded. Over the last decade or so many organisations have adopted a competency-based approach to selection and, in defining such competencies, have made use of them in the wider context of human resource management generally. Conversely, some organisations have adopted a competency framework for other purposes and then made it available for the selection activity.

Regardless of the origin, the important benefit is that there is a consistency in identifying and measuring 'people quality' at all stages in the employment cycle. The use of competencies is further discussed in Chapter 5 and for the present it is sufficient to say that it is the identification of skills, motives, personality characteristics, and other attributes which give rise to performance and which differentiate between poor, average and superior performance; expressed in plain terms as descriptions of the qualities in action in everyday work. Using the competencies means that it is not only possible to select against them, but to predict the workplace behaviours of the candidate and monitor performance against them, aligning performance management and training programmes to support and enhance optimum performance. Thus the creation of a competency-based specification provides clear, quantifiable measurement of people; it allows the principles of total quality management to be applied to the management of human resources. Since a properly prepared person-specification will have been generated from thorough role analysis, it also means that there is very clear information about the roles within the organisation, their purpose and contribution to the overall business aims. Figure 2 illustrates how the identification of competencies can feed into many different HR processes.

Human resource planning

Effective human resource planning must begin with an analysis of the needs of the business in order to identify the requirements of people within it, both in terms of numbers and the role required. Good planning needs to be soundly anchored in reality, since it is not an end in itself – the art of prediction – but an integral part of human resource management, setting the demand for the strategies that will be put in place. There is therefore a very close iterative link between HR planning and selection. The planning output will create the target for selection quantity and quality, in the sense of specifying the number and skills required and the type of people needed. In the course of planning, labour markets and movements will have been analysed together with other trends, and flows within the organisation will have been analysed in terms of promotions, labour turnover, retirement, etc. Sophisticated HR planning will also gather information on the causes behind past trends, for example research into reasons for leaving, in order to make meaningful predictions about future trends. Such information is of great importance to the selection activity since it will define the attractions and reservations influencing potential employees and applicants. In the

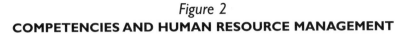

Figure 2
COMPETENCIES AND HUMAN RESOURCE MANAGEMENT

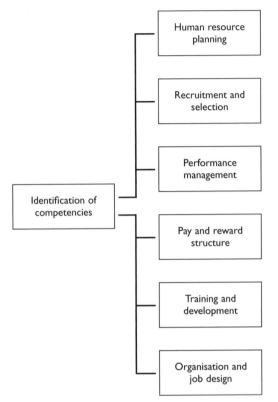

course of selection activity, information will come to hand about trends in the labour market which will be valuable to HR planners, along with information on the difficulties or ease of recruiting appropriate numbers and types. Thus information on selection ratios at each stage of the process can help HR planners to determine the viability of achieving increases or reductions in staff numbers through increased recruitment or natural wastage. In order to make decisions on candidates, information will have been obtained on their alignment with the person-specification; this information needs to be captured within an integrated human resource information system so that in making plans which will require certain levels or availability of skills, planners will be able to determine whether such skills are available from within the existing workforce.

Performance management

During the course of selection, a great deal of information will have been obtained about candidates and there should be clear measures of their competencies. This will be invaluable for both day-to-day general management of performance and the formal performance management process. The day-to-day management of performance will be enhanced by providing managers with a clear understanding of the nature of the people working for them, their potential and their limitations, their preferences and dislikes, what 'makes them tick' and ways to motivate them. Such information will allow managers to determine how much freedom of action can be provided to an individual, how much support they are likely to need, and to predict how they will cope and react in certain circumstances. Knowing, for example, whether someone is likely to be a risk-taker will help managers to see (in certain circumstances) that they will need to keep them on a tight rein and provide clear guidelines or limits on the degree of risk, or redesign the roles so that high risk elements are reallocated to more prudent people. In so doing, the manager may be informed, from the employee's selection profile, that he or she will perhaps dislike completing forms or perhaps will react adversely to close supervision, etc. Using all the information available, the manager is able to select the most appropriate course of action to avoid undue risk without adverse impact upon the motivation and performance of the employee. It has long been held that situational leadership – the ability to apply different styles of leadership to different types of followers in different circumstances – is the most effective form of leadership but it has been difficult for leaders to secure information on their staff which provides the indications they need to adapt their leadership style. The selection profile should provide this kind of data.

Formal processes of performance management, such as performance appraisal, suffer from some common faults. One of these is that the process favours senior people over junior people in the allocation of good performance ratings. It is a common occurrence in most organisations that receiving higher performance marking is far more likely for senior staff than for junior staff. One of the reasons is that the schemes themselves often provide fewer opportunities for junior staff to have their contribution fully assessed because there is a bias towards projects or one-off objectives. This means that managers and other senior people whose role is characterised by setting of goals and milestones, but where day-to-day standards and routine are less common, find that they can focus on clear goals and targets and be appraised against them. Junior staff, who have less discretion over the nature of the work, and usually less opportunity to become involved in projects or other goals, often find that the performance appraisal process overlooks the on-going, day-to-day, routines and standards which are important in maintaining the organisation's performance. Performance appraisals in many cases still seem to be derivatives of management by objectives. Competency-based appraisal processes provide a balance of targets (*what* is to be achieved) and behaviours (*how* it is to be achieved). This provides a more balanced system and can accommodate the differing nature of junior and senior work, since senior people will have more emphasis on the 'what' than the 'how', while junior people will have more emphasis on the 'how' rather than the 'what'. A competency-based appraisal system takes a balanced view of overall performance and will typically involve:

- setting targets for the role either in terms of specific projects or objectives, or other measurable dimensions of performance, such as volume of output or customers served or sales achieved
- behavioural descriptions of the standards expected in fulfilling the role, ie the competencies, which are expressed as agreed statements of behaviour at both 'expected' and 'advanced' level
- a development plan arising from the first two elements specifying any training or other development activities required to support the employee in achieving the targets and competencies

- a system of periodic review at quarterly or six-monthly intervals leading to an annual appraisal of performance against the targets and sustained achievement of the required competencies.

The selection process should be able to do two things. First, it should provide predictions on how the new employee is likely to perform, giving an assessment of how the individual will behave in comparison to the desired behaviours. Second, it will pin-point where areas of attention are required, ie potential weakness.

Pay

The payroll is often the most significant area of an organisation's expenditure. There is always the danger that it can be viewed as an overhead rather than an investment, with little attention being paid to how the organisation can maximise its return on such a large annual investment. It is true that legal obligations etc in practice provide little choice but to continue paying people on an on-going basis; the workforce is not truly a disposable component. Yet, although not 'avoidable', there is no reason why pay should not be expected to 'sweat'. It can be used as the foot on the accelerator or the brake. It can be used to push the motivational button and reinforce people's desire to achieve certain goals, or it can be used to press the stop button, to make people think twice about pursuing goals the organisation does not regard as important or displaying behaviours which it does not regard as desirable. It is not unusual in the design of pay systems to press such buttons accidentally. This occurs when there is insufficient information about the psychology of the people working for the organisation, and therefore little opportunity accurately to predict the likely outcome of changes to the pay system. To take an example: people who have a low locus of control (that is to say, they regard themselves as having little control over their own work environment or indeed any other aspect of their destiny) will see themselves as being unfairly punished if levels of pay are pegged back in a performance-related scheme (and bemused at being unnecessarily rewarded when payments are made) because they are unable to see how they could influence the outcomes upon which the pay is based. Performance-related pay will therefore rarely motivate such people, and will often de-motivate them. Conversely, those who have a high locus of control (ie they believe themselves to be firmly in charge of their destiny and in full control of all aspects of their work) will be favourably disposed to individual performance-related pay, but their attitude to team pay may range from indifference to loathing. In both cases the investment opportunity of the pay scheme has been diluted because the design has not been effectively aligned to the target group. Porter and Lawler's well-known model (see Figure 3) attempts to summarise all the factors which impact on pay's capacity to motivate.

Beauty is in the eye of the beholder, and the motivational aspect of pay is in the mind of the recipient. It is, of course, always possible and desirable for pay designers to undertake research as part of the design process. It is highly unlikely, however, that it will be possible to undertake the amount of detailed research on individuals which can be found in the selection process. Capturing the information which is gained on employees as part of the selection process, and feeding into decisions on pay design, will prove invaluable.

In addition to the 'soft' data, there are also the 'hard' data available to recruiters, on the sufficiency of the employment

Figure 3
PORTER AND LAWLER'S MOTIVATIONAL MODEL FOR PAY

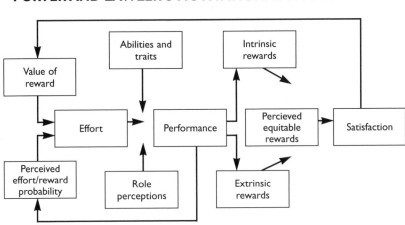

package to attract new candidates. Some care needs to be taken with this, given that poor recruiters will often blame lack of a competitive salary, rather than their own failings, as excuses for failure to recruit. Simple amendments to the application form asking for details, for example, of current salary can nevertheless provide some very good raw data for development of local pay intelligence.

Training and development

The use of a competency-based approach to human resource management means that measures of individual ability can be more precisely and objectively defined. It is possible to build up a very robust analysis of individual training needs from the performance management process as described above, and of course the individual training plan for induction and early development can be tailored precisely to the needs of the new employee. Equally, collective training needs can be gathered from the output of the role analysis, contrasted with the aggregation of data from individual competency-based assessment. Since the role analysis and the person-specification are expressed in exactly the same definition of competencies, it is possible to be very clear and specific in targeting the shortfall. Using the framework of competencies, it is also possible to see where the training and development investment is likely to yield the greatest return. Natural competencies (ie the deep-seated underlying personal characteristics) are less receptive to training and development interventions, and expenditure in such an area can be regarded as extravagant. Similarly, in looking at whether the 'deficiencies' are in the acquired or adapting competencies, it is possible to see whether they would be better served through education (for acquired) or training and development (for adapting).

There is an element of a two-way street here. It should not be assumed, in making selection decisions, that deficiencies in acquired or adapting competencies are less important than those in the natural cluster because training can be provided. It may be the case that such training is not available, or is prohibitively expensive, that it may be 'cheaper' for the organisation to accept lower levels of performance from someone deficient in natural competencies but sufficient in acquired and adapting competencies, than to select someone with sufficient natural competencies but deficiencies in acquired and adapting competencies. To take an obvious example, it would be unwise to choose the company legal adviser without legal qualifications, or a typist without typing skills, on the basis that their judgement, resilience, and interpersonal skills are excellent and the 'shortfalls' are capable of being trained. These may be farcical examples but they should serve to make the point that recruiters and trainers need to be in close liaison to ensure that they are aware of, and supportive of, each other's demands.

Integration

Some organisations choose to adopt a competency framework as the architecture for their human resource policies and practices. In so doing, they define the competencies required in the organisation that can be used for selection purposes as the specification, and the recruitment activity can be subsequently 'bolted in' to the framework. Some organisations choose to begin with the recruitment function, developing competency-based people-specifications as the basis for selection, and then use the specifications as the framework to drive other HR practices. The starting point is not important, but it is important that integration takes place and that:

- selection of people into the organisation is tied into the needs of the role
- the induction and development of people is built around such demands for the role and their compatibility with it
- pay creates the connectivity between the needs of the business and the values and expectations of the workforce
- the requirements of the role are clearly explained to those undertaking it
- insights into those people are clearly conveyed to those responsible for managing them.

Furthermore, decisions on the design of the organisation will need to take account of the character of the current workforce, and so too will plans for any future change.

Outsourcing

Organisations face a choice on whether to resource the recruitment and selection function internally or externally. Where outsourcing occurs, it generally takes one of two forms:

- using an external agency to undertaken all the functions expected of an internal recruitment and selection department
- contracting-out individual assignments as required.

There are many examples of entire sections of staffing being contracted out to agencies, eg typing services. In such cases, however, it is often the case that the organisation has contracted-out the services rather than the recruitment function, ie the agency selects and employs the people and charges the organisation for the service, rather than selecting the people for the organisation to employ.

There are no hard-and-fast rules as to why a recruitment function should or should not be resourced in-house. It is simply a matter of management decision taking account, as in any other decision, of cost, convenience and suitability. It is true that in theory internal recruiters will be more familiar with the business and the personalities, but in practice they can sometimes be more remote and less supportive than an outsourced agency, which is acutely aware that its existence is dependent upon the quality of service provided. Equally, it should be the case that specialists are able to provide a higher-quality or lower-cost service than an in-house team, but it is often the case that in-house teams can provide higher levels of proficiency, innovation and technical expertise at lower cost than some external specialists. The key considerations will therefore be:

- is there likely to be sufficient frequency or volume of recruitment and selection to justify an in-house function?
- can the organisation afford the salaries of a skilled team or the training expenditure to bring generalist staff up to speed?
- are there any sensitivities or information about the organisation which need to be closely guarded?

Table 1 sets out a more systematic method of analysing the issue.

Table 1

OUTSOURCING THE HUMAN RESOURCE FUNCTION

The Institute of Personnel and Development, together with the Chartered Institute of Public Finance and Accountancy, and the Society of Chief Personnel Officers in Local Government published a guide to evaluating the quality of outsourced providers in the context of compulsory competitive tendering. They suggested assessing on a points system based on:

• know-how and experience	20 points
• access to specialist data and advice	15
• acceptability and relevance of proposed methods	15
• compatibility of style with the organisation	20
• price	30

An analysis of the issues is provided by Alan Fowler in *People Management*, February 1997.

Recruitment consultants

It is possible to outsource *ad hoc* assignments to a recruitment consultant. At one time recruitment consultants were used mainly for specialist or senior appointments where a particular expertise was not available in-house. Nowadays their use is more widespread as human resource departments have faced cut-backs and changed their role from being 'providers' of service to 'procurers' of services. Similarly, many organisations have devolved human resource management to line managers who will not have the time or expertise to cope with recruitment 'blips'. There are three main ways in which consultants are used:

- registers
- selection
- search.

Registers were traditionally restricted to temporary agencies (and similar) maintaining a database of candidates sourced primarily from their own advertising. The significant advantage of this approach is that candidates were pre-screened and available fairly immediately. In more recent years their use has widened so that agencies are now very significant in, for example, the recruitment of IT staff (albeit that many provide them as a contract of services from the agency rather than helping the organisation to recruit them). The incidence of executive redundancy has created interim databases of experienced managers and professional staff capable of undertaking short-term assignments. Many large-scale redundancy programmes have been assisted by out-placement consultants who have developed a database of redundant staff and who have been proactive and professional in marketing their services to prospective organisations. Many specialist recruitment agencies maintain a database of candidates seeking new employment, since they are aware that many organisations express a sense of urgency when assignments arise.

Selection consultants may be assigned to a specific project, eg specialist managers or professional staff, and will work with the client to take (or help develop) a clear brief of the candidate, make all the necessary arrangements for advertising, receive applications and screen them on behalf of the client, and provide the client with a shortlist of recommended candidates, usually accompanied by a report on each. The benefits of using selection consultants are their ability to devote time to the urgent task, their knowledge of the market and how and where to begin advertising etc, their professionalism, and (where required) the opportunity for the client to remain anonymous.

Search consultants operate differently from selection consultants (although many provide both kinds of service) in that selection consultants aim to hold out the job as an attraction for suitably qualified people to apply, while search consultants actively seek out those people with a view to persuading them to work for their client. Using the search approach can be particularly appropriate where there is a small pool of people with potential suitability for the role. Thus, it has tended to be restricted to executive and very specialist positions. The advantage of using the search method is that it is more targeted, and more proactive than simply relying on appropriate people to apply. The downside is that it can be expensive, carries high discrimination risks, and is very dependent upon the skills and network of the 'head-hunter'.

The costs of the three approaches vary; the register method can cost from 10 per cent to 30 per cent (of the employee's first year's salary), depending on the availability of, and demand for, skill. Selection consultants normally operate on a fee equivalent to about 20 per cent of the first year's earnings of the selected employee. Search consultants generally charge a fee of about 40 per cent of the first year's earnings. Some consultants charge fees on the basis of time spent rather than related to the earnings of the person recruited, and will apply the charge regardless of the assignment's success. Consultants charging a fee linked to the employee's salary will often only charge (apart from expenses) where the assignment is successful. There is, of course, always the opportunity, though not always taken, to negotiate the scale of fees.

In choosing consultants, care should be taken to check out their suitability. It may be appropriate to look at their track record and seek out references on them but, even with satisfactory commendations, their method of operation should be carefully checked since professionalism is not always present. In particular, check:

- that the consultant will undertake to prepare a detailed specification to form the basis of the selection assignment and which will be agreed with the client
- that guarantees are provided on time-scales, with penalties if appropriate
- that all elements of decision-making, including screening applications and interviewing will be undertaken by the consultant rather than 'delegated' to junior untrained staff
- that all candidates will be treated courteously, paying particular regard to the acknowledgement of applications, advice on progress, and promptly notified of decisions
- that all ethical and legal requirements are fulfilled and the client is indemnified for any liability incurred
- that proper methods are used to make the selection, including the use of structured interviews, tests, and other techniques

- that they undertake not to 'poach' appointed people at a later stage, or in any other way breach the confidence or trust of the client
- whether they will undertake all appropriate checks such as references and verifying certificates and qualifications claimed.

It is not out of order to quiz consultants and agencies on these points since they will be the outward face of the organisation and, however confidential the assignment, will at some time cause candidates to connect the reputation of the client organisation with the standards of the consultant or agency.

4

EQUAL OPPORTUNITIES
AND DISCRIMINATION

Discrimination

Discrimination is the essence of recruitment; it is about trying to discern and segregate the suitable from the unsuitable and it is not always 'fair' in that employment invariably is given to those suitable to perform the task rather than the most needy. It may not be 'fair' to offer the job to the candidate who is already in employment, or who has a number of alternative offers, over the candidate who is unemployed and has no work alternative. The duty of selectors is to ensure the most appropriate selection rather than to redistribute social justice. There are, however, certain groups in society facing unfair disadvantages and prejudices, and whom the law seeks to protect. The law does not attempt to provide such groups with an unfair advantage, rather it attempts to ensure that there is a level playing-field so that they may receive proper consideration in applying for positions. The law directly precludes unfair discrimination based on sex, race, disability or criminal history. It indirectly precludes discrimination on the basis of religion (directly in Northern Ireland) and in some cases on the basis of age. From a legal perspective there are three main ways in which discrimination can take place:

- direct discrimination
- indirect discrimination
- victimisation.

Direct discrimination, as the phrase implies, is where someone is discriminated against directly because of one or more of the unlawful factors. Thus, permitting only white males to be considered for a particular role would directly discriminate against non-whites and women. *Indirect discrimination* occurs where an act, although not discriminatory in itself, has the effect of discriminating against key groups. So, reserving employment for people with blond hair and a beard is likely to be indirect discrimination against non-whites and women because, by virtue of their race or gender, they will be far less likely to fulfil the criteria. It will not be indirect discrimination against men even though dark-haired clean-shaven males are excluded; they will not be excluded because of their gender since a significant proportion of men will be able to fulfil the criteria. Discrimination by *victimisation* occurs where someone is treated less favourably because they have committed a protected act, ie brought proceedings or assisted in bringing proceedings or complaints under equal opportunities laws. The significance of whether the discrimination is direct or indirect is that the penalties and remedies are greater for direct discrimination.

The main purpose of the discrimination legislation is to ensure that people are not treated less favourably in their employment by virtue of belonging to one of the appropriate groups. The legislation therefore covers most aspects of the employment relationship, including terms and conditions and pay. Unlike other aspects of the law which provide rights to people only during the employment contract, the legislation on discrimination extends to those seeking employment and therefore has significant relevance for recruitment and selection.

Sex

The Sex Discrimination Acts 1975–86, and associated regulations, make it unlawful to discriminate because of the person's sex – whether male or female – in employment, union membership, education, provision of goods, services and premises, and advertisements for the same. Although disparity in pay and conditions between male and female employees is covered under the Equal Pay Act, disparity in offers of pay and conditions to prospective employees are covered under the Sex Discrimination Act. There are cases where it is legitimate to discriminate on grounds of sex where it is a 'genuine occupational qualification', for example actors in a play, where the work involves personal services to individuals promoting their welfare or education, where the job requires living in, where the job is at a single-sex institution such as hospital or prison, where the job is one of two to be held by a married couple (such as running a public house), where it involves close physical or social contact with the employer, or where the job is in a country where the laws or customs forbid it to be undertaken by a woman. There are also some special provisions in the Act for occupations such as police, prison officers, ministers of religion, midwives and mine workers.

Direct discrimination

There are very few cases of direct sex discrimination as a result of earlier cases such as *Thorndyke* v *Bell (1979)* which shows that it was discriminatory to refuse employment to a woman because of family commitments, and *Horsey* v *Dyfed CC (1983)* where it was discriminatory to refuse secondment to a woman on the assumption that she would leave and follow her husband to a new place of work. Even 'sympathetic' discrimination is still unlawful, as in *Greig* v *Community Industry (1979)* where the woman was refused employment 'in her own interest' as the only potential female in the work group.

Indirect discrimination

Although there are nowadays very few cases of direct discrimination, indirect discrimination has shown itself in a number of ways, some obvious and some very subtle. It is probably the case that most indirect discrimination is also unintentional and may be the result of customs and habits which have not been properly thought through. Indirect discrimination is established if four conditions are fulfilled:

- there must be a requirement or condition applied to all applicants
- that condition or requirement is such that the proportion

of women or married people who will comply with it is considerably smaller than the proportion of men or single people (and vice versa)
- the condition is not justifiable
- it is detrimental to the complainant because he or she cannot comply with it.

There is some difficulty with the legislation in that some criteria for recruitment are not necessarily regarded as 'a requirement or condition'; they must an absolute bar rather than merely guidance. Conversely, whether people 'can comply' is not whether it is theoretically possible but whether it can be reasonably expected. In the case of *Wylie* v *Dee (1978)* a menswear shop claimed that the requirement for a man was a genuine occupational qualification because the job could involve taking inside leg measurements. It was held that there was no real likelihood of customers objecting to a woman doing this and, even if there were objections, there were other male assistants who could be called upon to help. In *Price* v *Civil Service Commission (1977)* a requirement that applicants should be between 17 and 28 years old was indirect discrimination because it was an arbitrary age requirement with which many women could not comply because it was affected by child-bearing years. One of the likely sources of complaints of indirect discrimination is the nature of questions at an interview. Although the complainant will still be required to show that the reason that he or she did not get the job was because of discrimination on the grounds of their sex, citing dubious questions would help to establish some degree of proof. More pertinently the Equal Opportunities Commission, which was established under the Sex Discrimination Act, has issued a code of practice which advises against asking such questions as whether the person is thinking about marriage or starting a family etc. The code is not legally binding but it is taken into account by courts and tribunals in reaching their decision.

Pregnancy
Pregnancy is a somewhat difficult area. The Employment Rights Act 1996 renders all dismissals on ground of pregnancy automatically unfair, regardless of length of service or whether

the contract is indefinite or for a fixed term, but the Act applies only to people currently employed. It does not apply to recruitment. The purpose of the amendment to the legislation in the Employment Rights Act was to clear up confusion in the way the Sex Discrimination Act was applied.

For recruitment purposes, however, legal uncertainty still prevails. This is because some tribunals have interpreted the rules by making comparisons between the way an employer would treat a pregnant woman and a man on long-term sickness. Yet it has also been argued that there can be no comparison between a pregnant woman and a man, of whatever condition, because men cannot become pregnant. The significance of this rather tenuous debate is that, if there is no comparison, discrimination is direct, whereas if there is comparison then discrimination is indirect. This has a bearing on the nature and scale of the remedies available to the woman refused employment.

Sexual orientation
Discrimination on the grounds of gender re-assignment is unlawful because it is based on sex (*P* v *S & Cornwall County Council 1996*). Discrimination based on sexual orientation is not outlawed under the provisions of the Sex Discrimination Act or any cases arising from it. In the case of *Saunders* v *Scottish National Camps (1981)*, dismissal of a homosexual maintenance handyman (although not in contact with the children or alleged to be a paedophile) was held to be fair because other employers would have acted the same way – a curious and perhaps volatile reasoning. Different treatment between gay men and women will, however, be discrimination on grounds of sex, not of sexual orientation. Unlawful discrimination against people with AIDS is probably covered by the Disability Discrimination Act 1995 although, through careless drafting, this cites HIV, not AIDS, as a progressive disability and as a possible impairment to employment.

Race
The Race Relations Act 1976 makes it unlawful for an employer to discriminate on the grounds of race in the

arrangements made for the purpose of determining who should be offered employment, or on the terms on which employment is offered, or in refusing or deliberately omitting to offer employment to an individual. The Act also makes it unlawful to publish or cause to be published an advertisement which might reasonably be understood to be an intention to discriminate, regardless of whether that act of discrimination is actually unlawful. The latter point means that job advertisements suggesting that any particular race or group will be either excluded or preferred will be unlawful. The Act makes it quite clear that discrimination is on grounds of race not of ethnic minority. White Europeans are covered to the same extent that ethnic minorities are covered.

Direct discrimination

Direct discrimination occurs even if it is through others. Thus, in a number of cases brought in 1995 against concessionaires in Harrods Store, pressure brought by Harrods on the concessionaires, to discriminate against people on grounds of their race, was direct discrimination. Although the act was committed by the concessionaires, the system of 'store approval' caused the discrimination. Similarly the 'victim' can be discriminated against on racial grounds even though that 'victim' may not be of that race; thus in *Zarczynska* v *Levy (1979)* a barmaid was directly discriminated against when she was dismissed for serving a black customer against her employer's instructions, and in *Wilson* v *TB Steelwork Company*, a white woman was refused employment because her husband was black and this was held to be discrimination on racial grounds. As with sex discrimination, 'sympathetic' discrimination is still unlawful. In *Din* v *Carrington Viyella (1982)* and *Albertie* v *Ace Minicars Ltd.*, discrimination because of racial tension in the workplace was unlawful, and was similarly unlawful in *R* v *Commission for Racial Equality ex parte Westminster City Council (1984)*, where the Council attempted to eradicate prejudice by the appointment of a black man which resulted in threats of industrial action, in consequence of which the appointment was withdrawn.

Indirect discrimination

Indirect discrimination is more likely, not simply because employers may be less open about their discrimination but, more likely, because of unthinking actions that have the undesired effect of creating discrimination. Thus, in *Isa & Rashid* v *British Leyland Cars*, Pakistani candidates were indirectly discriminated against because they were required to complete application forms in their own handwriting; they could not read or write English and, as candidates for labouring jobs which did not require an ability to write, this was unlawful. In *Hussein* v *Saint Complete House Furnishers (1979)* the employer advised a careers officer that he did not want anyone from a certain area of Liverpool, but since 50 per cent of the population in the area was black, compared to 2 per cent for the surrounding areas, it was held that the condition was indirectly discriminatory. In *Perera* v *Civil Service Commission (1982)*, the applicant was denied access to promotion to a certain grade because he was over the age limit of 32. It was held that the applicant had been indirectly discriminated against because he was Asian and many people of Asian origin did not come to work in the UK until they were of a mature age, and would therefore be less likely to comply with the age requirement than UK-born candidates.

Victimisation

Victimisation occurs when an individual is discriminated against because he or she has brought proceedings or pursued or supported some form of action under the Race Relations Act. It must be clear that this is an action *under* the Act, so that reporting alleged race discrimination to a community relations council was not held to be an action 'under the Act' in *Kirby* v *Manpower Services Commission (1980)*. In *Ailia* v *Britvic Corona Ltd*, an Asian student was unlawfully victimised when refused temporary vacation work because he had previously given the company 'too much of a hard time' in an earlier employment spell in which he had complained about segregated rest rooms and complained to the local Council for Racial Equality about the employer's discriminatory employment practices.

Disability

The most recent legal development in outlawing discrimination has been in the area of disability, enacted by the Disability Discrimination Act 1996. The Act withdrew the previous arrangements for employing quotas of disabled people and reserving certain employment (such as lift attendants and car park attendants) exclusively for disabled people, and developed new legal definitions of disability and coverage for discrimination purposes. The Act defines disability as:

- a physical or mental impairment
- which must have adverse effects which are substantial
- the substantial effects must be long term
- the long-term substantial effects must adversely affect normal day-to-day activities.

Although registered disabled people will come under the scope of the Act, its coverage is not limited to those registered as disabled. The definition of employment for the purposes of the Act extends to cover all full-time, part-time, temporary, and self-employed workers. There are statutory exceptions for police, prison officers, fire fighters, and Services personnel. Disability discrimination does not have the concepts of direct and indirect discrimination which apply to both sex and race discrimination, but it does outlaw victimisation which, as with race and sex, can apply to non-disabled people. The Act does not apply to employers of 20 or fewer people.

Discrimination

It will take a number of years for sufficient cases to be heard and appealed, to create a body of case law to give examples. There is, however, a code of practice which provides hypothetical examples which will be taken into account in making judgements. The Act, together with the code, provides a wide-ranging scope of discrimination applying both to employees and applicants for employment. Thus there is discrimination arising not only from the disability but from a reason relating to the person's disability, for example problems related to a wheelchair or a guide dog. Unlike the Sex and Race Discrimination Acts, the Disability Discrimination

Act permits positive discrimination in favour of disabled people. The Act also requires that any arrangements made by an employer, or any physical feature of premises occupied by the employer, which place the disabled person at a substantial disadvantage compared to the non-disabled should be remedied by the employer or potential employer. Such steps include:

- making adjustments to the premises
- altering working hours
- assigning to a different place of work
- acquiring or modifying equipment
- providing a reader or interpreter
- providing supervision
- allocating some of the disabled person's duties to another person
- allowing absence during working hours for treatment, etc.

In a similar vein to other discrimination legislation, the Act makes it unlawful to discriminate against a disabled person:

- in the arrangements made for determining who should be offered employment
- in the terms in which employment is offered
- in refusing to offer or deliberately not offering employment.

It is similarly unlawful to discriminate against disabled employees in the opportunities afforded for promotion and availability of support such as training.

The primary purpose of the Act is to protect those who are discriminated against because of their disability and thus it incorporates disfigurements such as scars, birthmarks and skin disease (although these need to be 'severe') and progressive conditions having 'substantial' adverse effects (whether currently or having such an effect in time). Examples of progressive conditions specifically mentioned in the Act are multiple sclerosis, muscular dystrophy and HIV infection.

The Act may not be as carefully drafted as one would wish, and there are some curious consequences which may be addressed in future years. It is, for example, unlawful to discriminate against someone whose disability affects their work, but seemingly lawful to discriminate against someone where their disability does not affect their work. This is particularly the case with progressive conditions where, for an action to be unlawful, symptoms must have already begun to emerge. This would mean that screening applicants for cancer, multiple sclerosis and muscular dystrophy before the occurrence of symptoms, or genetic screening for illness, and subsequently rejecting the candidates who tested positive, would be lawful. Conversely, wholly innocent acts may give rise to discrimination claims; thus where an applicant is called for interview and decides not to attend because he or she sees steps to the premises which they would not be able to negotiate in their wheelchair, the potential employer would be deemed to have discriminated by not making appropriate arrangements (if the employer had information which indicated the likelihood of such disability, eg questions on the application forms).

Justification
Unlike other discrimination legislation, the Act allows an employer to justify discrimination on grounds of disability if there is justification which must be 'material to the circumstances of the particular case' and 'substantial'. The code of practice gives an example of someone disfigured with a severe skin condition which renders them unsuitable to model cosmetics as part of a job. Conversely, choosing a 'fast' typist over a 'slow' typist would be discriminatory if the 'slow' typist was slow because of an arthritic condition and speed of typing was not a substantial feature of the job. Similarly, not being able to get a wheelchair up steps, or to operate machinery, because of a disability will require the employer to make adjustments, where reasonable, to remove the disadvantage.

Possible discrimination
There are some other areas which, though not wholly or specifically covered by dedicated legislation, may give rise to legal liability.

Religion

The Fair Employment (Northern Ireland) Acts of 1976 and 1989 outlaw religious discrimination in Northern Ireland as a consequence of discrimination between Catholic and Protestant religious groups. Discrimination on religious grounds in the rest of the UK is not directly legislated against but is protected against in some cases through the interpretation of the Race Relations Act and, in all cases, through Article 9 of the European Convention on Human Rights, to which the UK is a signatory, and which guarantees the freedom of thought, conscience and religion, including the freedom to manifest one's religion or beliefs. The Sunday Trading Act 1994 provides protection for employees not to be dismissed for refusing to work on a Sunday (for religious grounds) but permits discrimination against applicants who would not be available for work on Sunday (but protects them if they start work and subsequently 'change their mind').

A London Policeman who was not allowed to swap shifts to avoid working on Friday nights and Saturdays, in pursuit of his Jewish faith, was claimed to have been discriminated against under the Race Relations Act. Rules prohibiting long hair may discriminate against Sikhs, who cannot be discriminated against for not wearing safety helmets (conflicting with the religious duty to wear turbans) because the Employment Act 1989 gives them exemption from statutory requirements to wear safety helmets.

In defining 'ethnic groups' for protection under the Race Relations Act, religion plays a major part. Although the Law Lords have identified two essential characteristics of an ethnic group, namely:

- a long shared history, of which the group is conscious as distinguishing it from other groups and the memory of which it keeps alive
- a cultural tradition of its own, including family and social customs and manners.

They go on to quote other characteristics such as:

- a common religion different from that of neighbouring groups or from the general community surrounding it.

This means that gypsies were seen to have a common ethnic origin because they were descended from Hindu origins (which by reverse logic would suggest that Hindus would be regarded by the courts as an ethnic group) and Jewish people also constituted an ethnic group. There have been cases that hold Muslims are not an ethnic group, but this has yet to be challenged in the higher courts and, in the case of *J H Walker Ltd* v *Hussain & others*, the Employment Appeal Tribunal (EAT) found there to be discrimination against a large number of Asian employees, nearly all of whom were Muslims, when the employer refused holidays during a Muslim festival. The EAT stated that direct discrimination against members of a particular faith may also amount to indirect discrimination against members of a particular racial group.

Age

Although it is 30 years since the USA prohibited discrimination in employment on the grounds of age, there is as yet no legislative control in the UK on age discrimination. There is mounting opposition against age discrimination, however, and in 1995 *People Management* declared that it would no longer carry advertisements which discriminated on the grounds of age. There is, of course, legitimate age discrimination both in terms of statutory minimum ages for employing young persons and in allowing for termination of employment upon reaching retirement age. There is no direct law to prohibit age discrimination but this does not always mean that it will be lawful. While there may be no legal 'right to work', the common law laid down in *Nagle* v *Fielden (1966)* and *Langston* v *AUEW (1974)* indicates that opportunity for employment should not be subject to arbitrary restrictions. Furthermore, age can be seen as a form of indirect discrimination, as in the case of *Perera* v *Civil Service Commission* which held that age limits could work against immigrants who might be older than British citizens by the time they gained relevant qualifications, and in *Price* v *Civil Service Commission (1977)* where requirements for applicants to be 'between 17 and 28 years old' indirectly discriminated against women who could not comply because it affected child-bearing years.

Crime

The rehabilitation of Offenders Act (1974) permits a convicted person to become 'rehabilitated' after a certain period, which in effect means the conviction becomes 'spent' and gives the person certain rights. The person will not be required to disclose the conviction and is entitled to say, in response to any request for information on criminal convictions, that they have none. Furthermore, the conviction, once 'spent', cannot be used as a reason for rejecting the applicant. The length of 'rehabilitation' varies from six months to 10 years dependent upon the penalty imposed, but convictions resulting in imprisonment for more than 30 months are never spent.

There are exceptions to the Act, particularly professions such as doctors, nurses, midwives, dentists, barristers, solicitors, accountants, teachers, policemen and directors of building societies. The Act is excluded from any office or employment concerned with the provision of accommodation, care, leisure and recreational facilities, schooling and social services, or supervision or training of, persons under 18, which would involve access to such minors in the ordinary course of employment.

Trade union membership

The Trade Union and Labour Relations (Consolidation) Acts 1992 makes it unlawful to refuse a person employment because of his or her membership, or non-membership, of a trade union, a particular union, or part of a union. The provisions are wide in their effect and can apply not just in situations where someone is rejected following an application and interview or test, but there could be 'refusal of employment' by failure to respond to a telephone call or speculative letter. The Act also applies to situations where a trade union puts forward or approves only persons who are members of the union, and discriminates against a non-member.

Positive action and positive discrimination

Not all discrimination is negative. There are occasions where employers may take steps to remedy an under-representation of a particular group within the workforce. Positive action occurs when an employer attempts to remove the barriers perceived by the discriminated group, for example by ensuring that advertisements or notices are placed in areas where under-represented groups may see them. Positive discrimination occurs where there is direct action to give more favourable treatment to the under-represented group by, for example, giving preference to Asian candidates over their white counterparts. Positive action is legally permissible, whereas positive discrimination is not.

Equal opportunities

Practical steps to avoid discrimination
It can be seen that the focus of legislation against discrimination is not only on advertising and decisions on offering employment but also 'in the arrangements that are made for the purpose of determining who shall be offered employment', which of course means the recruitment and selection practices and policies. While overt discrimination due to prejudice may be tackled through statements on equal opportunities and by appropriate training, it is the case that ingrained or unthinking discrimination needs to be engineered out of the process through careful attention to recruitment practices.

Objective requirements
The development of the person-specification needs to be undertaken thoroughly, taking care to avoid description of the previous incumbents, but rather focusing on the key requirements of the role itself. Taking care to avoid arbitrary qualifiers such as age, qualifications, experience or physical attributes inessential to the role will help to create a realistic and balanced profile. The use of a carefully-drafted competency framework related to the key requirements of the role, identified through a proper role analysis and expressed in objective descriptions, will provide a very solid platform.

Fair and open competition
The employment *marketing* strategy should ensure that any advertising or promotion is not confined to media which may

be less accessible to under-represented groups, and indeed efforts should be made to take positive action to ensure that opportunities are brought to the attention of such groups. Open recruitment practices are less likely to be discriminatory whereas 'word of mouth' recruitment through existing employees, restriction to internal appointment only, recruiting through families of existing employees, through trade unions, etc, have all been condemned as methods of perpetuating the current composition of the workforce and are therefore likely to be discriminatory. The content of any *advertising* or recruitment literature needs to portray an image of a mixed workforce and should show a balance of ethnic groups, males and females, various ages, etc. Care needs to be taken to avoid showing that higher positions are occupied only by white males, and similarly to avoid showing sporting or other 'physical' images which suggest that disabilities will be a bar. This is not to suggest that advertisements ought not to be imaginative or 'catchy'; there is, however, a tendency for imaginations to run riot, particularly in graduate recruitment, where pictures of mountaineering may be intended as a metaphor for ambition but which may suggest a requirement for physical attributes and fitness wholly unrelated to the reality of the training programme. Similarly, perpetuating the 'milkround' in certain universities or favouring candidates from certain public schools may be seen to be practices discriminating against women or ethnic groups. Statements welcoming applicants from under-represented groups should be included in the advertisement through phrases such as 'we seek to be an equal opportunities employer and welcome applications regardless of age, gender, race or disability'.

Suitable application procedures

The method of application should be constructed so that it is free from discrimination. Requiring applicants to complete forms 'in your own handwriting' has the potential to be discriminatory against those whose first language is not English or against the visually impaired. Where standards of English or reading are required as essential elements of the role, then of course it is quite justifiable to incorporate such aspects, but for roles where it is not required, or where adjustments can be made for a disability, then the practice should be avoided. Similarly, the content of the application form should be framed around essential elements of the role rather than 'nice to know' aspects. Asking questions about certain experience or 'GCSE grades' may imply an intention to discriminate which may not actually be present. The development of biodata screening methods should ensure that the construct measures (ie the factors which differentiate) are not discriminatory and that the questions are not framed in a way that assumes a 'western' education or lifestyle, or predominantly a male or female disposition. Telephone screening will need to take account of those with speech or hearing impairment, particularly if it is not a requirement of the role, and alternative avenues may need to be offered. The importance attached to information gathered for making shortlisting decisions must, of course, take account of alternative backgrounds and lifestyles. Paying attention, for example, to speed of promotion may discriminate against women and ethnic minorities facing greater difficulties in achieving such progress due to the very effects of discrimination.

Proper testing
The use of psychometric tests, and especially ability tests, is a particular cause for concern. It is important to ensure that the test itself is not discriminatory and, in choosing tests, employers should carefully check that the test has been tried out on samples of female, ethnic and disabled groups to ensure that it is free of bias. Particular care needs to be taken to ensure that the ability that the test is measuring is an essential prerequisite of successful performance in the role for which the person is being recruited. Many cases of unfair discrimination have been raised because of the indiscriminate use of ability tests, particularly for literacy or numeracy, where such abilities are not relevant to the position being filled. Consideration will also need to be given to helping disabled candidates to complete the test if their disability renders it difficult to do so.

Balanced and objective interviews

Care needs to be taken in the interview regarding the choice of questions and consistency of questions. The Equal Opportunities Commission and the Council for Racial Equality have both issued codes of practice which will be taken into account in deciding claims of discrimination, and which advise against certain questions which might indicate an intention to discriminate. Asking female candidates about how male colleagues would respond to them, or about their plans to start a family, or about childcare arrangements, may indicate the presence of discrimination. Similarly, asking ethnic minority candidates how white colleagues will react to them, or about their right to work in the UK may be seen to be discriminatory. Even 'off the cuff' conversational questions can cause concern, as in the case of an Irish candidate who was asked questions about Guinness which was perceived as racial stereotyping on alcoholism and detrimentally affected interview performance. Given that the Disability Discrimination Act requires employers to make provision to assist disabled persons to perform their role, it may be necessary at the interview to phrase such questions carefully around the help that is needed rather than around the challenges or obstacles faced. It is highly unlikely that anyone will be more acutely aware than the disabled person of the challenges that he or she must surmount. It is an effective interviewing technique to maintain consistent questions and this can be particularly helpful in avoiding discrimination; a question which it would be embarrassing to pose to an able-bodied white male is one that probably ought not to be asked of any candidate.

Care should also be taken with certain kinds of interviewing; it has been shown that situational interviewing (where candidates are asked to say how they would respond to a hypothetical situation) tend to be discriminatory in making it difficult for people whose first language is not English to respond effectively with the grasp of abstract language and concepts. Body language is, at the best of times, a concept of dubious authenticity; all the more so in the interview of minority candidates. A well-qualified black female teacher was discriminated against as a consequence of an 'unsuccessful interview' because of failure to make good eye contact with her interviewers, but the Employment Appeal Tribunal accepted the evidence that people of Afro-Caribbean origin often avoided eye contact with those in authority, such eye contact being regarded as impolite. In some ways the employer is 'between the devil and the deep blue sea', in that questions about the right to work in the UK would be seen to be discriminatory, but on the other hand employers would be liable for employing someone who needs, but does not have, a work certificate (regardless of whether the employer knew that they needed such certificate). Good practice may, however, be to incorporate this element into the status checks at the offer stage, rather than in the interview.

Suitable exercises

The use of exercises and work simulations needs careful consideration to ensure that the exercises themselves are not incapable of being performed by, for example, disabled people (particularly highly physical outdoor-type activities) and that the purpose of the exercise is not to elicit information which may be discriminatory (for example, looking for aggressive behaviour in team leadership exercises). Where work simulations are involved, arrangements will need to be made to adjust the workplace, equipment etc, to accommodate disabled candidates.

Objective decisions

The basis upon which decisions are made must also be free from discrimination. One of the more common mistakes in making decisions about candidates is stereotyping, and racial stereotyping is one such example. A carefully-drafted person-specification or, better still, a clearly-defined competency framework, will provide an objective benchmark against which selectors may measure candidates rather than relying on subjective criteria. Additionally, training interviewers and decision-makers in equal opportunities principles and in ways to avoid discrimination are good investments. Providing interviewers with examples of model answers to questions in addition to examples of non-discriminatory questions can help eliminate bias, and the use of a consistent scoring mechanism, properly applied, is particularly effective in eradicating selection bias. Particular attention should be paid to avoiding over-emphasis on how the candidate will 'fit in' with the existing workforce, particularly where 'fitting in' means a different gender, racial background etc, from the current work group.

Offers
While legislation on discrimination forbids such discrimination in the process of recruitment and in the decisions on recruitment, it also extends to the terms on which employment is offered. Care must therefore be taken to ensure that there is consistency because there will still be a successful claim if the terms are rejected by the applicant. Thus, a female student hired for a temporary holiday job as a security guard was unfairly discriminated against by not being offered night shifts, which resulted in loss of earnings (*Dunlop* v *Royal Scottish Academy*). Similarly, applying employment regulations in a certain way may also be discriminatory. For example, forbidding women to wear trousers has been seen to be discriminatory to Sikhs and Muslims, particularly where there is more hardship for the applicant to adhere to the rule than for the employer to change it. Conversely, while rules against wearing beards have discriminated against Sikh men (whose religion requires that they should wear them) it has been ruled justifiable where employers of food products insisted on the rule as part of their hygiene standards.

Induction
Sadly, the workplace is still an environment where abuse can be manifested through sexual and racial harassment. Care needs to be taken, therefore, to monitor the induction period (and beyond) to ensure that such abuse does not take place and that the new employee is integrated smoothly and effectively into the workplace.

Monitoring
In addition to engineering-out the potential causes of discrimination, on-going vigilance will need to be maintained through the monitoring of equal opportunities. The development of an equal opportunities policy, and training in it, will

be a worthwhile investment. Candidates who are likely to suffer discrimination need to be identified and an equal opportunities monitoring form should be incorporated into the selection system. Such a form, seeking information on the candidate's sex, race, disabilities, religion (in Northern Ireland), and age should be used to gather information on the success of certain groups at each stage of the selection process. By using the information it will, for example, be possible to assess whether ethnic minority candidates have as much chance as others in proceeding to and beyond the short-list stage, whether the failure rate at testing is disproportionate and whether interview scores are consistent with other parts of the process. Such monitoring should be established as a regular and systematic part of recruitment activity and all assignments should be accompanied by such statistical analysis. Collecting the information on the form can be a cause of concern or sensitivity and it is better collected on a form separate from the application (or a detachable portion) with an explanation to candidates of the purpose to which the information will be applied. An example appears in Table 2. The Commission for Racial Equality and the Equal Opportunities Commission provide guidance on ways to monitor equal opportunities. There is no similar organisation established under the Disabilities Discrimination Act but local Disablement Resettlement Officers (contactable through the local Job Centre) would probably be willing to offer advice.

There is always a danger that equal opportunities will be seen as a 'right thing' to do; a moral obligation which needs law and activists to promote. The reality, however, is that the natural law of distribution dictates that there must be sufficient numbers of perfectly suitable candidates among different sexes, races, religions, political convictions etc, to warrant full and proper consideration. Given that it is always difficult to find good candidates, it makes sound economic and business sense to give full and fair consideration to all candidates – or selectors will have failed to perform their role properly.

Table 2
EQUAL OPPORTUNITIES MONITORING FORM

We do our best to promote equality of opportunity and to ensure that people are selected for employment on the basis of their suitability and are treated fairly, regardless of race, sex, marital status, disability, age, religion or any other aspect not related to job performance. We need to be sure that we deliver on our promises, so we use this form to check on progress. The form is not used for selection purposes but to monitor the decisions made, and to ensure they are made fairly. Please help us by completing it.

Name: ....

Post applied for: ....

Location: ....

Are you: Male   ☐   Female   ☐

                Single   ☐   Married   ☐   Widowed/Divorced ☐

                Black-African   ☐
                Black-Caribbean   ☐
                Black other   ☐
                Indian   ☐
                Pakistani   ☐
                Bangladeshi   ☐
                Chinese   ☐
                White   ☐
                Other (specify) ....

                Age   under 30 ☐   30–45 ☐   45 or over ☐

                Disabled ☐
                Any special facilities needed to attend interview? ....

                ....

Signature .... **Date** ....

Part 2

REQUIREMENTS

5

PEOPLE–SPECIFICATIONS AND COMPETENCIES

Specifications

Selection has been described as finding a needle in a haystack. Maximising the effectiveness of selection is therefore not only about improving the methods of removing the hay but also about improving the recognition of the needle. One of the difficulties of selection has always been the subjectivity of decision-making. It is an area in which many selectors feel uncomfortable and it is also the source of greatest disagreement between those undertaking the selection and those on whose behalf they undertake the assignment. Such disagreements can take place between a selection consultant and the client, or between the personnel adviser and the line manager.

The information technology (IT) industry many years ago recognised the problems inherent in vague and loose approaches to defining requirements for new systems, which often led to a breakdown in relations between the IT providers and their customers, and leading to overly-expensive or under-performing solutions to IT needs. The IT people responded by placing great emphasis on detailed specifications of customer requirements so that there was a clear understanding of the requirements, the solution, and the deliverables, before any work commenced. Such a slow and measured approach can seem alien to recruitment, in which the nature of the exercise is a more rapid event, usually requiring a quick recruitment of the new person to the organisation and, on the face of it, a lower cost issue with far fewer players involved. After all, in most IT projects other people will be involved in maintaining or using the system, its impact can spread widely, and it may need further amendment from time to time. It is, however, not unrealistic to consider selection in similar terms.

In the same way that the IT designer is unlikely to be the person operating the new system, so too will the selector be unlikely to be the person managing the new recruit. In the same way as the IT system may potentially have a wide range of end-users or recipients of the information, so too in today's organisations will the new recruit be networking widely and interacting with a great number of customers, both internal and external, and be relied upon for information and service in the same way as many IT systems. Nor are there many IT systems that compare with the cost associated with the employment of people, both in terms of salary and related employment costs spread over the average length and service with the organisation. Coupled with the knock-on cost of the decisions they make, or the services they use, the high-spend on IT projects can pale into insignificance, particularly for more senior appointments. It is unlikely that many IT projects, pound-for-pound on a par with selection expenditure, measured in such terms, would go through 'on the nod and wink' and the informality which accompanies many selection assignments.

Person-specification

One of the problems of selection is that of 'mirroring', in which selectors often choose candidates who mirror their own values, beliefs, abilities etc, rather than stepping back and searching for the candidate best suited to their client. Good selectors adopt the practice of drawing up a clear specification of the ideal candidate and agreeing the specification with those on whose behalf they undertake the assignment. Such a specification needs to be very comprehensive and embrace not only the skills, background and experiences of the ideal candidate but also the individual qualities and working style of such people. By drawing up an agreed specification, the chances of success are much improved, not only because of the inherent improvement to the process of selection but also because the likelihood of subsequent disagreement between selector and the client is thereby minimised.

A useful approach is the PERSON-specification covering:

- **P**ersonal qualities and attributes which are inherent in the person's character, not easily changed, and pertinent to good work performance. Does the person need to be creative, or resilient, or be able to follow detail and routine, or be 'good with people'?
- **E**xperience, whether of a particular industry or type of work, or dealing with certain types of customer, etc.
- **R**ecord of achievement or evidence that the potential has been applied and realised, eg projects completed or sales achieved.
- **S**kills or qualifications needed to perform the role. Some roles may necessitate certain qualifications, eg law or accountancy, perhaps as a statutory requirement, others may have a specific requirement, eg driving licence, or qualifications may be used as a guide, eg degree-level.
- **O**rganisation-match, which may cover the fit with the style and culture of the organisation if it is significant (perhaps very 'laid back' and informal or perhaps very formal and bureaucratic) but more usually aspects such as shift-work or travelling requirements.
- **N**eeds and expectations of the candidate; what does the organisation require?, eg someone looking for a long-term career, someone looking for a short-term fill-in, someone wanting routine or someone seeking new challenges?

Care must be taken to prioritise between essential and desirable requirements and to avoid any form of discrimination. 'Physically fit' may be a requirement for a professional sports player, but incorporating it into the specification for a sales representative may create an offence under the Disability Discrimination Act 1996. Similarly, specifying the requirement for 'O' levels has been found to be race discriminatory. Similarly, the use of stereotyped personal qualities such as 'assertive' or 'aggressive' may be deemed to be sex discrimination. Great care needs to be taken, therefore, to incorporate aspects that truly relate to job performance and are objective and defensible. Although the use of informal approaches such as PERSON-specification can help in odd cases as a better option than 'I'll know it when I see it', it is a poor substitute for proper role analysis. Undertaking role analysis and adopting a competency-based approach to selection will significantly improve effectiveness, objectivity and fairness.

Using competencies

In recent years the development of a specification has become much easier due to the use of a competencies approach.

The competencies approach was developed in the 1980s and 1990s as a way of providing the measurement of people which is so elusive in day-to-day human resource and general management. Two approaches took different paths at similar times. In the UK, greater integration within the European Community and moves for greater mobility of labour across the EC necessitated the definition of national qualifications and skill levels for meaningful measures and comparisons across countries. This was accompanied by a concern bordering on embarrassment about the levels of skills in the UK, particularly in managerial roles where it was felt that the acquisition of management skills was much more haphazard than in other European nations; in particular it was perceived that in Germany many managers were highly qualified and skilled. In the UK the pattern had been for people to drift into management through the 'University of Life' , gathering experience and hopefully expertise 'along the way' without any underpinning of a formal body of knowledge or qualification in management.

To address the mobility of labour and portability of qualifications, the development of National (and Scottish) Vocational Qualifications (NVQs/SVQs) began. To put the art of management into a science with a professional standing, the development of the chartered manager began, which eventually became the Management Charter Initiative (MCI). These approaches received considerable government funding and support from large companies and academic institutions as well as government agencies. Since their primary concern was to ensure that standards were achieved and developed they became focused on training and development approaches, specifying minimum standards for achievement of set tasks and activities, expressed in ways that were capable of observation and assessment with a view to certification, and thereby qualification. Since an integral part of the approach was to provide the opportunity for people to receive training and development to achieve the required skill, it became necessary to break jobs down into significant detail and put in place an assessment process that was robust. This approach became rather bureaucratic and unwieldy and was the cause of much criticism in recent years, which has been addressed.

On a parallel time frame, in the USA a move was growing to improve the competitiveness of US industry. A highly successful management book called *In Search of Excellence* became influential and sought to examine successful US corporations and identify the recipe for their success, a recipe which could be adopted and copied by others. A natural extension of such an approach was to look at successful managers and see whether it would be possible to replicate their approaches and their qualities in others. The American Management Association commissioned McBer Associates to undertake research into successful managers and to attempt to identify their qualities and features. The consultant, Richard Boyatzis, concluded in his research there was no single factor but rather a range of factors that differentiated the successful from the less successful managers. He concluded that there was a variety of factors, including personal qualities, experience, motives, and various other attributes.

Boyatzis coined the term 'competency' (plural competencies) originally used by Harvard Professor David McClelland in his work on motivation. The term was defined as 'an underlying characteristic of an individual which is causally related to effective or superior performance in a job'. In the UK the term 'competence' was adopted (plural competences) to indicate the range of standards. The Training Standards Agency defined competence as 'an action, behaviour or outcome which the person should be able to demonstrate'. A summary of this distinction appears in Table 3 overleaf.

Table 3
DEFINITIONS OF COMPETENCES AND COMPETENCIES

Competences
Things that a person who works in a given occupational area should be able to do. Each one is an action, behaviour or outcome that the person should be able to demonstrate.
The Training Agency, *Definition of competences and performance criteria*, 1988

Competencies
Those characteristics that differentiate superior from average and poor performance . . . motives, traits skill, aspects of one's self-image or social role, or body of knowledge.
Richard Boyatzis, *The Competent Manager*, 1982

The difference between the UK and US approaches is more than simply words and phrases. It is a fundamental difference between looking at:

* a small number of key aspects which differentiate between performance regardless of whether they are visible or hidden, and
* looking at the full range of skills needed to perform a role, regardless of whether they differentiate between levels of performance, but confined to those aspects which can be observed or assessed (and therefore trained and developed) in people performing the work.

It is a difference between drivers of performance and standards of work. The US approach does not confine itself only to the observable aspects but also includes the underlying values or characteristics which contribute to performance. The US approach does not look at all the requirements of the role, merely at those which differentiate between levels of performance.

Although this broad distinction is fairly clear cut, the approaches have tended to merge in UK companies, and sometimes the loose use of the language masks or confuses the real nature of the approach. This has often occurred because many of the UK companies adopting the approach were themselves subsidiaries of US corporations, and their adoption of the competencies route came through their parent organisation rather than from the external business world. Often it is a mix of the external influence and the internal customisation that has led to a hybrid approach. In practice, neither approach should be regarded as inappropriate since they both have something of value. A pragmatic route is to adopt both approaches but to be very clear on their use. Using the 'competence' approach has limitations for selection since it places an emphasis on looking at people doing the work, and on the assumption that with sufficient effort they can be trained and developed to do the work. In such an approach it is therefore implicit that there is little point in differentiating at the time of selection and that the effort should be placed on training and developing people for whatever role for which they can be equipped. This has some serious limitations in practice. The US route can be particularly helpful in making selection decisions because it is looking at the underlying characteristics which may not yet have had the opportunity to surface in an entirely similar environment, and it is therefore concerned with potential rather than accomplishment. The limitation here, however, is that selection is about bringing in people to do a job of work and it is important to know about the way in which they will perform. It is useful, therefore, to have a framework of competencies which accepts principles from both the US and the UK route. Such a framework can look at the natural, acquired, adapting, and performing competencies.

Competency framework

The true potential of the competency approach can best be exploited through accepting rather than rejecting the disparate approaches and codifying them into an integrated balanced framework. The language of the framework is not important; the classification is the critical element since it facilitates a practical balanced system for managing competencies.

The *natural* cluster would be all the 'underlying traits', to use Boyatzis' term, and thus the 'big five' dimensions of personality (see Chapter 10), namely

- extraversion/introversion

Figure 4
COMPETENCIES FRAMEWORK

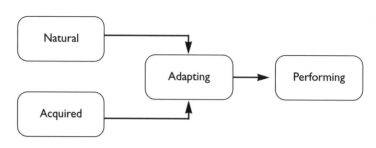

- emotional stability
- agreeableness
- conscientiousness
- openness to experience.

The *acquired* cluster would include knowledge and skills, whether achieved through work or elsewhere, with which people are not naturally gifted. Thus, professional knowledge or business awareness would be found within this cluster.

The *adapting* cluster forms the critical set which enables the individual to succeed in his or her work environment. All too often people in a new position fail to continue their previous track record of success. This can be true of highly-rated people failing to make a transition to a new department or organisation, or of people being promoted. Whether coming to terms with a different culture, a different operating environment, or a different set of priorities or demands, success will flow from the ability of the individual to adapt their natural talents and acquired knowledge to current circumstances.

The *performing* cluster consists of the observable behaviours and outputs that flow from the other three clusters. A framework showing how all these clusters fit together appears in Figure 4 above.

Overcoming criticisms
Using this structure, there is an identifiable framework of cause and effect. The management of competencies becomes clearer and the main criticisms are addressed:

- *Cloning*; the criticism aimed at the competency approach generally, and MCI specifically, about defining a single, prescribed way of operating is overcome by recognising the *adapting* elements. Using Kirton's Adaptive-Innovative scale, which places people on a continuum ranging from highly-adaptive to highly-innovative, such adaptation can extend to completely new management approaches and ideas.

- *Know-how*; there is an argument that in some roles or occupations, *what* the person does is more observable but less important than *how* they do it or what they *know*. In such situations greater weight can be applied to the *acquired* and *adapting* clusters.

- *Personality*; over-emphasis on observable behaviour ignores the personal characteristics necessary for success. Behaviour can be transient and is sometimes more a reflection of the environment than the person; although important for gauging current success it is not a reliable predictor of future success in a different arena. Recognising the importance of the *natural* cluster provides the appropriate balance.

The key message is that the management of competencies requires a broad view. In practice there is a tendency to flexibility. Even those who insist on restricting the definition to observable behaviour include competencies such as 'judgement' or 'resilience' which are more easily recognised as personality traits than behaviours.

Competency-based person-specifications

Preparing the specification in the form of competencies ensures that both the selector and the client have a clear understanding of the person being sought, and a clear agreement on what is meant by those terms. It can often be the case that selector and client have failed to agree that the candidate possesses a certain quality when there is no common understanding of the quality itself. Take, for example, looking for 'flexibility' where the client's view of flexibility may mean the willingness of the person to perform tasks outside the normal range of duties, and not to be too rigid in their outlook, whereas the selector's view on flexibility may be the ability of the person to undertake a number of tasks in different areas, or to switch easily between routine and complex tasks. Neither is incorrect in their view of flexibility, nor is either perhaps incorrect in their assessment of the candidate's flexibility. The difficulty is that 'flexibility' for one is different from 'flexibility' for another. Thus the benefit of taking a competencies approach is that people can identify and isolate the key characteristics which would be used as the basis for selection, and that those characteristics will be described in terms which both can understand and agree. Furthermore, using the description of behaviours of the competencies in everyday work, it is possible to identify good and bad answers to interview questions or good and bad responses to assessment exercises. Table 4 gives an example of how a competency framework can define different levels for each of the key competencies; they can then in turn, as here, be broken down into different levels of performance.

The competencies therefore become a fundamental part of the selection process. They become the technical terms for the specification in precisely the same way that the IT professional will use technical terms to describe the software being developed on behalf of his or her client. A further benefit of a competencies approach is that it breaks down the specification of the candidate into meaningful parts so that elements of the selection process can be best aligned to identify it and the whole process can be used to build a complete picture, component by component. This avoids the difficulties of 'whole picture' assessments, in which selectors are trying to make an overall judgement of a candidate but are not able to specify clearly the elements where they believe the candidate may or may not fit the requirements of the role. This often shows itself in concerns about subjective judgements of candidates and inevitable 'school report' type of assessments.

Using a competency framework it is possible to target the particular elements of the selection process so that, for example, the natural competencies that are deep-seated can become the focus of psychological testing which is most appropriate for identifying some of the underlying characteristics, the application form can be used to gauge the appropriate experience or

Table 4
USING COMPETENCY FRAMEWORKS FOR SELECTION

In this example, a company decided to profile a family of sales roles against a defined set of competencies. Some are inevitably more critical for some jobs than for others. One competency common to them all is *planning and organising*, which is defined as:

> The ability to plan, schedule, organise, prioritise, monitor and control work in the short and/or long term, ensuring effective use of time, money and resources to meet objectives.

Each competency is then divided into a set of levels (in this case, six), in which higher-level jobs usually – but not always – have higher-level competency requirements. Thus, an ordinary salesperson needs level-3 skills in *planning and organising*, a senior salesperson level-4 skills, and a sales manager level-6 skills.

Level 4 is described as follows:

> Able to set short-term plan of action to achieve goals, clearly able to prioritise and schedule multiple tasks and appointments.

Level 6 is defined as:

> Able to organise large team, set priorities and co-ordinate plans and actions to achieve medium-term (18 month) goals.

At every level, however, people are expected to demonstrate different standards of performance, in this example *threshold* for newcomers to a job, *proficient* for experienced employees, and *superior* for those hoping to progress. Behavioural examples are then used to illustrate what these might mean in practice. (Other organisations may feel able to make do with a rather less elaborate system.)

Here, in the case of *planning and organising* (level 4), *threshold* performers are expected to 'use the *xyz* planning system to prepare monthly priorities, a weekly call schedule and daily activity lists; to keep the *xyz* customer-log up to date and to send the follow-up papers to sales admin. twice weekly'. A *proficient* performer, meanwhile, would normally need to do all of the above, and to 'maintain key-customer activity analysis to monitor targets and develop six-month plan'.

knowledge of the candidates, and assessment centre exercises can be used to gauge the behaviours in performing. This therefore uses each technique to its best advantage without techniques competing or conflicting, and creates better overall pictures of candidates. Sometimes the selector will prefer one approach to another. They may, for example, think that psychometric tests are the best means of assessing candidates and will therefore place a heavy reliance on the psychometric techniques, even for those elements which may be better gauged by other means. So, too, there may be those who distrust techniques such as psychometrics and prefer to stick to interviews or perhaps references, and may then place undue emphasis on those elements and fail to recognise information coming from things such as the psychometrics. The pity is that all of these techniques are useful for gauging certain things and should be considered as good evidence for certain elements and rejected as insubstantial evidence for others. Breaking the specification into competencies means that the appropriate technique can be used to gauge *that* competency, and the overall picture is built up on a piece-by-piece basis and becomes more reliable. Figure 5 gives an example of how this works. Because the decision-making competency is here the most crucial requirement, the organisation uses two separate methods to check for its presence.

Figure 5

TECHNIQUES TO CHECK FOR DIFFERENT COMPETENCIES

	Screen	Test	Interview	Exercise
Achievement		✔		
Leadership				✔
Creativity		✔		
Resilience		✔		
Flexibility			✔	
Technical knowlege	✔			
Judgement		✔		
Decision-making		✔	✔	
Planning and organisation				✔
People management	✔			
Energy			✔	
Financial acumen				✔

In addition to providing the built-up picture, using the competencies enables the correct answer to be applied. While it is not suggested that selection should be seen as a test which candidates pass or fail, it is nevertheless the case that selectors, particularly those who undertake the task only occasionally, need to have some benchmark against which to measure. They need to know whether answers are good or bad in the sense of whether they provide evidence that the candidate possesses the competency in depth or not at all. Similarly, in using structured techniques such as psychometrics there is a need for some form of benchmark.

A further benefit of the competencies approach is that it becomes the thread extending beyond simply the selection process. The recruitment of the candidate should be only the first stage in the on-going relationship, is not an end in itself. All too often selection processes are seen as a discreet activity, the appointment of the individual being the culmination of the process. Thereafter the information is filed away with the rest of the assignment information and does not form part of the further development of the appointed person. In using the competencies approach it is possible to give the new manager information about his or her recruit which specifies how they are likely to perform against each of the competencies. In describing the output of the assessment in terms of the performing behaviours it becomes easier for the manager to see how his or her new recruit will perform. It will therefore provide the basis upon which their performance in the early days can be monitored to assess whether they really live up to the predictions flowing from the selection process. It is also the case that rarely does the ideal candidate step forward, fully meeting all of the requirements of the role. There are often compromises to be made or choices to be effected. By using competencies it is possible to show how the candidate broadly fits the specification but that there are some areas in which they are exceeding the particular requirement for that competency and other areas where they may fall short. In this way their induction can be planned so that attention can be paid to providing additional help, whether in the form of training, development or additional guidance to address shortfalls, or, if such shortfalls cannot be made good, ways in which the role can be redesigned, perhaps with additional supervision or a change of duties, to compensate and adjust for the deficiency in that particular competency.

The greatest benefit of a balanced framework is the practical application it affords for a system of integrated human resource management.

Natural competencies will have their focus in the selection process. The possession of innate qualities, as every selector knows, will not guarantee that the person will successfully apply his or her talents, but selecting people with the raw ingredients is an essential pre-requisite. Attempting to train or artificially create such natural talent is unrealistic. Also, it becomes easier to make the right decisions about which selection technique is appropriate for each cluster.

Acquired competencies may be a centre of attention for some selection decisions, but are also important as the focus for education. There is likely to be increasing emphasis on education in future years as the role of management shifts from direction and control to decision-making and communication. This may cause a reversal of the trend of recent years by making specialist and technical skills more valued than general management skills. The focus of NVQ and SVQs should be more clearly directed at *acquired* competencies within a balanced framework.

Adapting competencies should be used as the focus for development activities since this is the accelerator which the person uses to apply his or her natural abilities and knowledge or experience. Adaptation can therefore embrace the full scale from innovation to regulation and include cultural fit, commitment to corporate goals, team working, and decision-making. Since this is the point at which the person 'chooses' whether to apply the *natural* and *acquired* competencies, it is the area where development activities can have the greatest leverage in enhancing performance.

Performing competencies are already the focus of much attention as the observable behaviours and evidence of performance. It is the area most frequently covered in competency frameworks. These are useful as the basis of evaluating performance (albeit of greater use where measuring output-based activities rather than quality-based activities such as professional advice) and can provide a common language for objective appraisal and feedback. They can also provide the basis for designing organisation and human resource systems such as appraisal and reward.

6

ROLE ANALYSIS

Techniques

There are various techniques available to undertake the analysis of roles and to identify the competencies underpinning successful performance in a role. Since a clear specification will form the foundation for effective recruitment and selection, it is important that the development of the person-specification is robust.

The choice of technique will depend upon the resources available including time, and the preference, or expertise, of the identifier. A traditional approach to developing the person-specification is for the selector to meet with the client to identify key requirements of the candidate, paying attention to aspects such as qualifications, skill and experience. These may include formal qualifications indicative of general attainment, such as a degree, or they may be very specific job-related qualifications such as membership of a professional association. Background information on the kind of experience, and perhaps the industry sector or work nature, will also be needed together with the profile of the personal qualities that the candidate will bring to the work. Such aspects are covered under the PERSON-specification in Chapter 5. Using the competencies framework, described in Chapter 5, it is useful to think in terms of:

- the natural competencies, ie the personality characteristics of the candidate, taking care to focus on those which have a direct bearing on the successful performance of the role, rather than on 'desirable' or pleasing aspects of personality

which may appeal to the selector but which provide no
sound basis for influencing judgement

- the acquired competencies that will encompass formal
  education levels, job-related qualifications, and appropriate
  experience, be it the type of organisation or the type of
  work or both

- the adapting competencies which will look for evidence of
  how the candidate has applied himself or herself in his or
  her career, paying attention to the range of experiences or
  achievements which they should record.

Drawing up the specification in this way is useful to ensure
that the selector has a clear understanding of the client's
requirements, and it provides greater focus for the selector in
investigating and making decisions. It is a very quick and easy
method and will enable the selection process to get under way
without undue delay. The drawback is that it may be very subjective, and there is a danger that the selection will focus on
aspects that are not necessarily the key drivers of performance
or, at worst, are inappropriate to successful fulfilment of the
role. Taking a more measured and structured approach to identifying the profile through role analysis will pay dividends in
delivering a more robust specification and in securing the right
candidate. There will however be recruitment delays if this is
undertaken and this is the reason why many organisations
undertake general research into the framework of competencies
for their organisation, which is then available in readiness for
any selection activity (and other human resources actions).

Techniques for analysing roles to identify competencies
include activity-based techniques such as:

- focus groups
- inventories and questionnaires
- interviews including critical incident
- diaries and work-logs

and people-based techniques such as:

- repertory grid
- observation
- testing.

Focus groups

Focus groups involve bringing together a group of subject-matter experts to analyse roles and identify the key competencies underpinning successful performance in those roles. The usual approach is for the group to meet on a periodic basis, the frequency of which depends on the size of the organisation and the task but it usually entails fortnightly meetings over a period of months. The focus group will look at a cross-representation of roles in the organisation. It is customary to define the roles which cover about 80 per cent of the work population. The group will look at the roles, usually through a presentation by a member of the group, and focus on the key elements. The presentation will typically include a statement of the main purpose of the role, the key accountabilities for the role (usually about six to eight) and then the principal activities which flow from those accountabilities. This provides the group with an understanding of the nature of the role and its deliverables. The latter is usually best acquired by seeking performance indicators for the role, (ie the measures of how the role is successfully fulfilled) attempting to use objective yardsticks. Using this information, the group will then 'brainstorm' the range of qualities needed to perform the role. By looking at each role in turn, without reference to the other roles at this stage, the group will develop a pattern of qualities or competencies. When all the roles have been reviewed, the group should list all the qualities that have been identified, and then using postcards or post-it notes, sort them into clusters. There is no hard and fast rule on the number of clusters, although it is most effective to have as small a number as can be effectively handled (ie remembered) by line managers. This is usually about six to eight. Some organisations use several dozen competencies but the reality is that, in day-to-day work, line managers find such a list far too cumbersome to deal with. The clusters should be of aspects that are similar to each other. Once the clusters have been identified, the focus group will then provide a working title and a definition for each competency, together with 'behavioural indicators' of the competency in action in everyday work.

One of the great advantages of using the focus group is that the titles and the language used in the definitions will be

Table 5

COMPETENCIES REQUIRED FOR BAND I ROLES AT THE COUNTRYSIDE COMMISSION

Key skill	Examples of expected behaviours	Examples of advanced behaviours
Judgement Absorbing and analysing data to identify trends and causes. Making effective decisions based on sound analysis of available options with independent thought and objectivity.	• Makes decisions based on set standards and procedures. • Refers or seeks advice when decision is outside set procedures or precedent. • Prioritises work to meet needs of job. • Uses resources of time or equipment etc to good effect. • Asks questions at the right time and looks for information and advice from the right places.	• Re-prioritises own work to meet changing demands. • Identifies problems in own work area and offers workable solutions. • Anticipates problems, and plans to counteract them.
Adaptability Adapting, responding to or innovating working practices, changing style or priorities to meet varying demands.	• Shows a willingness to adapt to new methods of working. • Prepared to take on different tasks. • Readily helps colleagues. • Switches easily from one task to another. • Copes with changing priorities. • Not afraid to ask questions to clarify understanding.	• Actively seeks to improve ways of working in own area. • Thrives on challenges and changes.
Influencing Understanding and using relationships within the Commission, with partners, and other organisations to gain commitment to shared objectives.	• Explains when and how a task can best be completed. • Communicates in a clear, concise and constructive manner based on own knowledge and experience. • Knows when to push a point and when to give way or compromise.	• Anticipates and understands other people's needs and sees their point of view.

acceptable to the end-users rather than employing the jargon of consultants or psychologists. By using subject-matter experts, ie those people who understand and perform the role, the analysis of roles is also thorough. Great care needs to be taken in selecting the focus group to ensure that it is representative of roles across the organisation, both vertically and horizontally, and particular care needs to be taken to ensure that the make-up of the group is not distorted on age, race or sex such that the competencies are in danger of being inherently discriminatory. One of the most significant difficulties with the focus group is securing the release of good quality people for the duration of the project. Table 5 shows some of the competencies required for roles at a certain level (Band 1), as generated by a focus group at the Countryside Commission.

Inventories and questionnaires

Where jobs are well defined and predictable in terms of the tasks and activities required, it is useful to use the inventory (sometimes called questionnaire or check-list) technique. This approach takes the range of job requirements and breaks them into segments of key tasks which are then sub-divided into day-to-day activities. This breaks the role down into a very significant degree of detail; an activity could, for example, be described as 'checking, coding and registering invoice'. The range of tasks and activities is usually developed by observing the jobs in action and discussions with job holders and/or managers. There are some proprietary check-lists which may form a short-cut in appropriate circumstances. A preliminary range of attributes or competencies is developed from the observations and interviews. A questionnaire is then developed to seek information from the job holder on the criticality of the tasks and information from the manager and/or job holder on the link between the competencies or attributes and the tasks. This is achieved by asking the job holder to rate, against each of the activities, a score for elements such as:

- the time taken to do the work
- the complexity of the work
- the consequences of error.

The ratings are then multiplied so that the greater the amount of time taken and the greater the complexity and the consequence of error, then the greater the overall rating for that particular task will be. This analysis provides us with the criticality of the tasks. The next stage is to rate, on a matrix, the importance of each competency or attribute to the performance of each of the activities. This is most usually undertaken by the manager of the job holder rather than by the job holders themselves, since this provides a more authoritative view of the required attributes. In practice, however, it is very useful also to gauge the job holder's view, preferably in discussion with the line manager, to provide a closer-related and balanced assessment. The importance of the competency is then determined by totalling the scores for the competency against each of the tasks; the rating may cover a scale from 'not required' to 'essential'. Thus, for each activity the rater is saying how essential that particular competency is to performing the activity.

The activities are weighted according to the criticality score. The sum of the scores then provides the rank order of importance of the competencies. This can be a very useful technique for gauging the views of a large number of job holders without the cost and inconvenience of focus groups or of extended interviews or observation. Although the check-list can look intimidating, a very comprehensive inventory can be completed within about 45 minutes. The greatest time taken is of course in analysis, for which a statistics software programme is essential. The nature of the technique, in looking in detail at the job requirements and involving a large number of job holders and managers, is very effective as an objective and robust measure. It can also be useful in predicting the competencies needed for a changing role by re-allocating and re-modelling the frequency or criticality of tasks for the future design of the work. A further advantage of the inventory approach is that it provides a direct linkage between the analysis of the job and the competencies and attributes of the individual. In many of the other techniques the formulation of the key attributes of the competencies remains a dislocated process.

Critical incident

This technique involves interviewing job holders and/or managers and is focused on identifying specific events that form a critical part of the role. Interviewees are usually asked to describe recent experiences in their work and the interviewer will identify a particular occurrence, usually of some significance, and probe the interviewee on the actions taken and the outcome. Through the process of structured interviewing of a number of job holders or managers it becomes possible for the interviewer to infer the attributes and competencies which the job holder draws upon in order to deal successfully with the critical incidents. One of the important considerations here is that the interviewer is not concerned with identifying an exhaustive list of the full range of attributes and competencies required to perform the role, but is rather more concerned with those aspects which are used in the more demanding or challenging situations and are thus likely to be the differentiators between various levels of performance and coping. One of the advantages of this technique is that by focusing directly on the attributes and competencies, the normal difficulties of trying to make the transition between the analysis of the work and the identification of the competencies is overcome. The converse, however, is that there is less emphasis on an analysis of the work itself and therefore the impact of future changes on the person-requirements are more difficult to model and predict. The effectiveness of the critical incident interview is strongly dependent upon the effectiveness of the interviewer and it therefore requires a skilled interviewer, experienced in the application of competencies, to be able to draw out the key points successfully.

Diaries and worklogs

Diaries or worklogs involve the job holders in maintaining records about themselves over a period of time, from which the appropriate competencies may be deduced. There are two ways in which the approach can be used. The first approach is a diary system in which job holders log the activities they undertake at various periods throughout the day, either on a time sampling basis (ie at various time points in the day they enter the work on which they are engaged) or on a sequential basis listing down the times they start and complete each of their key activities. The second approach is a factor-based log which lists key criteria, perhaps in the form of competencies, and job holders are asked to record each time these are employed. For example, the list may contain perhaps 20 factors which may include elements such as decision-making and accuracy. These are listed on a pro-forma and on each occasion the job holder is required to engage in decision-making or accuracy, he or she will note down the date and time and the specific example of the work in which they are involved and which needed them to use decision-making or accuracy. In this process it is possible to log a number of factors being employed in one particular activity or time period.

Repertory grid

One of the key principles in using competencies is the requirement to differentiate between superior, average, and poor levels of performance. Repertory grid is a process by which the differences between performers is analysed in order to draw out the competencies that cause such performance differences. The repertory grid is undertaken through a series of interviews with managers. In the interview, managers are asked to place people in various categories of performance, usually poor, average, and superior. To assist in the process the interviewer usually uses a set of cards on which the names of the people are written. It is important in this process that the interview is framed around real people and real examples, albeit that they do not need to be current or concurrent. The interviewer prompts the manager to describe some of the examples of performance which differentiate between the superior, average, and poor performers. The interviewer will focus on certain elements, often taking a draft set of competencies, and probe the manager on the differences between the different people.

To use an example, the manager may be asked to look at the differences in the approach to planning work between different sets of people. The manager may be asked to identify two people who are excellent at such work, two or three who are average, and two or three who are poor. The interviewer will then start to compare in different permutations. The interviewer may ask how the excellent people do things that are similar to each other but dissimilar to the poor people. The interviewer may ask what it is that the excellent performers do differently from each other, but which one of them does in a similar way to a poor performer. Through this process, by constantly re-configuring comparisons and differences, it is possible to isolate and identify the behaviours which accompany performance at different levels and which differentiate performance. It may, for example, be the case that the approach to planning and organising is similar between the high and low performers but different between two high performers, and one would conclude that this is not a key competency in the sense of differentiating or contributing to higher levels of performance. Conversely, if the approach to planning was consistent among high performers and differed from the approach of poor performers, it would be a good indicator of a differentiator of performance, and therefore a key competency.

Observation

One of the relatively simple methods of job analysis is to observe job holders in the normal course of their work, often accompanied by unstructured interviews. In this approach the observer is able to see the work at first hand and witness the behaviours associated with varying levels of performance. The observer will need to be skilled in the analysis of competencies since he or she will be required to deduce the competencies from the activities being observed. It is, however, the least disruptive method from the point of view of job holders and managers, though there is a certain disruptive element in people standing around observing. Although the observation may appear to be 'informal' it will usually entail the pre-development of a checklist of important or critical behaviours which the observer will be using as a guide. The observation process can therefore often take the form of two stages; the first stage being the drafting of the various kinds of behaviours into a record form. The second stage is then using the form as the recording mechanism for the observation. The observation may focus on a time series, that is to say noting down the behaviours (now classified into certain key behaviours from the initial observation) being displayed at various times of the day. Alternatively, the check-list may take the form of the key behaviours being noted against each of the key activities into which the job has been broken down, in a similar fashion to the inventory approach. Where a large-scale observation study is undertaken using a number of observers, the development, agreement and training in the use of the observer checklist is very important.

Testing

An effective but sensitive approach to identifying the competencies is to use psychometric tests on a range of job holders, and correlate the results of the test with job performance, in order to identify differentiating characteristics. For this to work it is essential that there are measures of performance available which properly class poor, average, and superior performance. A group of people, spread across the different ranges of performance, is asked to complete a series of tests, usually comprising both ability and personality tests. The results of the tests are then compared with the performance rating, and significant correlations will identify the key competencies. Care needs to be taken in choosing the battery of tests and to ensure there is a sufficiently wide range of tests available to cover the broad spectrum of potential needs. It will not of course be possible to know which particular test is of use until the exercise has been completed, since the exercise itself will identify the key correlations. There may be many aspects which the test is able to identify but which do not differentiate between levels of performance. There is, however, an extra advantage in that the test battery provides not only the differentiators of performance but also some benchmark data on the existing population against which external people can be measured as a guide in selection. Thus, for example, an exercise of this nature undertaken for bank lenders:

- showed levels of numerical ability (though not differentiating between the performance of poor, average, and superior

lenders) higher than the average for the general population and subsequently used as an entry benchmark for selection
* identified a personality factor which differentiated between levels of performance and which became a key competency.

Suitability

Each of the techniques has its own advantages and disadvantages. One of the great advantages of focus groups, repertory grid, critical incident interviews, and check-lists is that people are involved in the process. The focus groups in particular involve people in *describing* the competencies as well as simply identifying them, and this ensures that the language used is appropriate to, and comfortable within, the organisation. The advantages of some of the methodical approaches such as check-lists, diaries and critical incident interviews is that they can be easily analysed and therefore both defended and modelled for predicting the outcome of future work changes. The advantage of 'open' approaches such as observation, testing and repertory grid are that they do not predetermine the outcome of the analysis by confining responses to predetermined formats, and they may therefore be effective in both picking up unexpected competencies and avoiding existing bias or prejudice. The advantage of the techniques that differentiate on performance such as repertory grid and testing is the ability to focus on the key aspects which matter from a performance perspective.

All techniques, however, have some disadvantages. Techniques such as observation and repertory grid need skilled practitioners to undertake them, but even then there is an unstructured leap between the activities undertaken and the competencies required; it becomes a matter of judgement, albeit skilled judgement, that is therefore open to the bias of the observer or interviewer. The disadvantage of techniques such as focus group and repertory grid, which rely upon viewpoints of effective performance, is that biases about the way in which jobs should be performed creep into the process. For example, in repertory grid a line manager may describe a 'better' way one job holder handles conflict whereas the 'poor' way, although not the style of the manager, may be just as effective. In a similar way, focus groups can highlight competencies which the subject-matter experts 'believe' are important but which may not in fact be key to successful performance. This is particularly pertinent in looking at sex bias where males may give undue emphasis to aggression and females may give undue emphasis to empathy. This is one of the reasons that it is essential to ensure that focus groups have a proper mix of sex, ethnic, disabled, and other groups. Some approaches can be particularly sensitive. This is often the case with testing, where people often feel threatened by the process, observation, where people sometimes feel uncomfortable at being watched, and diaries and worklogs, which are seen as an additional burden imposed by 'big brother'. Even inventories or check-lists which are likely to take no more than an hour to complete can be seen as intimidating.

The ideal approach is to use a range of techniques so that the end result is comprehensive and balanced. Equally, thought needs to be given to the outcome of each analytical method. Testing, for example, can be very effective in identifying potential as part of the selection process; it is very objective and the outcome will provide precise measures against which new candidates can be assessed. It will not, however, readily provide examples of the competencies in everyday behaviours. Focus groups, on the other hand, will be able to provide very useful detailed examples of everyday behaviours of the competencies in action, but not all of those examples may be useful in identifying potential within people who are being selected. The repertory grid will provide evidence of the key differentiators between the poor, average, and successful performers but will down-play or overlook the core standards which are essential for all levels of performance.

In looking at the way in which the job analysis can support the selection process, the most important aspect is that it develops a clear specification of the person being sought. This in itself justifies the investment of time and money spent in developing the analysis. It can, however, extend into direct support for the various selection techniques. An analysis based on testing will of course identify the most appropriate test to identify the differentiating competency and provide norms for benchmarking candidates. Where testing is to become part of the selection process this is therefore a highly valued method of analysis. The information from repertory grid can be very useful in developing the screening process, since the application form can be designed to draw out examples of experiences similar to those derived from the grid. The critical incident output, and often the focus group output, particularly behavioural indicators, can be very useful in providing examples of experiences to gauge interview answers and frame interview questions.

7

CHOOSING TECHNIQUES

There are numerous techniques to assist in the screening and selection of candidates, and choices will need to be made about which techniques to use. Descriptions of the techniques are given in the following chapters but the choice of any technique will need to based on:

- suitability
- resource or cost constraints
- effectiveness
- acceptability.

Suitability is concerned with whether the technique is appropriate for the specific aspect it is attempting to assess. Looking at qualifications, for example, will provide no indication of personality characteristics nor will measures of personality give an indication of expertise in a particular subject area; this is not to say that application forms or personality tests are not effective selection techniques, simply that they are effective only when applied to a suitable purpose. Consideration of resource and cost constraints may be an affront to purists looking at the effectiveness of techniques, but such is the reality of life in modern organisations that the proverbial 'coat' needs to be cut according to the cloth. This is not an entirely negative viewpoint, and it is sometimes the case that organisations adopt too great a sophistication in selection practices where clear focus and some basic techniques will provide a very effective selection system. It is important to look at the effectiveness or validity of any particular technique if reliance is to be placed upon it. Great emphasis is often placed by researchers on this particular aspect, often to the exclusion of any other consideration. Although important, in practice it needs to be considered alongside the other three factors. The acceptability of a technique is of great importance. 'Acceptability' includes acceptability to the client (whether a formal external relationship or an internal 'colleague' relationship), acceptability to applicants and candidates, as well as ethical and legal standards.

Suitability

It is important when choosing the technique to focus on the aspect which it is intended to measure. This becomes much easier when a competency-based approach is used. Using the competencies framework outlined in Chapter 5 it is possible to look at the most suitable techniques for natural competencies, acquired competencies, adapting or performing competencies. Natural competencies (ie the underlying personality traits and characteristics) can be identified through the use of personality tests or structured behavioural interviews. The acquired competencies lend themselves to identification through techniques such as the application form and curriculum vitae, ability tests, and structured interview. Similarly, work simulation or telephone screening can also be used to identify the acquired competencies. Techniques suitable for the adapting competencies include personality testing, structured behavioural interviewing, and structured situational interviewing. Assessment centres, which comprise a range of techniques such as testing, interviewing and exercises, can have individual components of the assessment centre targeted on natural, required and adapting competencies. Biodata are suitable for identifying natural, acquired and adapting competencies but the nature of the technique means that it is not possible to identify which particular competency (and therefore which particular type) is being identified, since it works on matching rather than analysis. Generally speaking, clearly defined requirements such as experience or qualifications which come under the acquired competencies are suitable for identification through explicit measurements such as application forms or straightforward interviews or tests of ability. The less visible aspects, such as personality characteristics which are to be found in the natural competencies, are better identified through indirect or subtle techniques such as testing. The adapting competencies are more suited to identification through dynamic techniques, such as interviewing, which enable elements to be explored on an interactive basis, but personality testing can identify the propensity to be adaptable, and assessment centre exercises and work simulations can attempt to replicate the real workplace dynamics.

Resources and costs

Selection techniques differ widely in their resource requirements and support costs. It is, however, important to look at costs in the complete sense of development costs, production costs, and usage costs. Consideration also needs to be given to whether the technique is to be used for screening or selection decisions since the number of applicants screened will usually be greater than the number of candidates being assessed in the final selection, and in some cases the screening process will need to deal with very high volumes.

Of the main screening techniques, curricula vitae have no development or production costs because such costs are borne by the applicant, but the usage cost is generally higher than application forms or biodata because there will be no standardisation of CVs and therefore screeners will be inefficient in screening because of the need to familiarise themselves with different layouts, and perhaps information will be missing. Application forms are generally cheap to design and produce, even if undertaken professionally, and although the final unit cost will be dependent upon the shelf-life of the form and the volume of applications processed, unit costs are usually measured in pence rather than pounds. Usage costs are usually lower than CVs because screeners can become proficient in finding and assessing the information, particularly where proper training is provided and a scoring system used. Biodata and telephone screening are higher-cost options. It is possible to develop a biodata form in-house, but it is more usual to employ consultants to develop one, and consultant fees for about 10 to 15 days would seem an appropriate guide for the total development costs. Printing costs will be on a par with application forms if scored manually, but where an option is undertaken to use light-reading machines, specialist printing will be necessary; this may edge the unit costs into pounds rather than pence. Using light-reading machines for scoring biodata necessitates a capital investment of usually a few thousand pounds, but since such a machine can score a biodata form in less than a second it can, with large volume campaigns, reduce usage costs to such an extent that even with all the development expenditure it becomes the lowest-cost screening option. There is also the opportunity to link the biodata scoring to applicant databases, word processing and mail merge software to further automate the administration of selection. Telephone screening has a high development cost, particularly where on-line scoring and appointment logging systems are used, since programmes need to be written, scripts prepared and telephone interviewers trained. Production costs are also high since call centres need to be staffed to respond to applicants, leading to equipment and staffing expenditure. The usage costs will be high because of the need to staff the call centres, and the overall costs of telephone screening can therefore be significantly higher than paper screening, running into unit costs of several pounds. There is, however, the opportunity to offset costs of later selection techniques such as the interview or to conduct the interview within the telephone operation.

The cost of assessment techniques can vary significantly, not simply because of the comparative costs of the techniques themselves but because for each technique there may be a variation in costs between different providers. Interviewing can be seen as a low-cost activity since most people are capable of establishing a dialogue with a candidate, but an effective interview will incur some cost in the development of an interview system and the training of interviewers, while the costs of the interview (effective or ineffective) will be significant because of interviewer time. These costs may be 'hidden' where internal resources are used, or explicit where external consultants are used. Unit costs of a one-to-one interview are expensive when measured in labour cost terms and the unit costs of panel interviews are, of course, significantly greater. Some organisations choose to develop their interviewing system in-house and provide training accordingly. Some organisations choose to use proprietary interview training costing a few hundred pounds or proprietary interviewing systems, which vary in cost from a few hundred to several thousand pounds.

The cost of psychometric testing varies widely. There are some published tests which are freely available and therefore cost nothing to develop or acquire. The most expensive option is probably the development of a bespoke test which could take a minimum of 20 days of consultant time. For larger organisations with in-house psychologist expertise and significant recruitment demands, this may, however, be a very cost-effective route. The cost of proprietary tests differs between providers but, generally speaking, ability tests are cheaper than personality tests – the former being in pounds, the latter being in tens of pounds. Some organisations sell their tests as single usage tests and charge a unit price, some provide reusable tests and charge a one-off purchase fee, others provide multiple usage tests but charge an annual licence. Costs are sometimes attached to the test itself, sometimes they are attached to the scoring system. In addition to the cost of the tests there is the cost of training. Organisations employing occupational psychologists will not incur additional training costs but for all others it is usually the case that The British Psychological Society rules will be applied, and users of ability tests will need to undergo Level A training of six days, and users of personality tests will be required to undertake Level B training for a further six days. In addition to the explicit test costs there are also the hidden costs of time spent in administration and scoring, although most scoring nowadays is computer based. It should be noted that training in test administration is provided to individuals, not organisations, and the loss of selectors can therefore necessitate further costs in the training of their successors.

Assessment centres are probably the most costly of any of the selection techniques because they usually comprise a combination of techniques. The design of the assessment centre can often represent significant development costs and, if undertaken by an external consultant, will take about five to 15 days consultancy, depending on the balance of original or 'off-the-shelf' material used. In addition to the development costs, there is a significant degree of training required for assessors, and usage costs are high because of the numbers of assessors used and the range of materials employed.

It is difficult to make a straightforward cost comparison between the various assessment techniques, but in simple terms it is fair to say that testing and third-party interviewing are high on 'hard' (visible) costs but light on resource requirements, whereas in-house interviewing is low on 'hard' cost but high on resource requirement, and assessment centres are high on resource requirements and medium to high on 'hard' costs.

Effectiveness

The effectiveness of any selection technique is of great importance since the amount of resource or cost devoted to it or the degree of reliance placed upon it must be influenced by its accuracy. It may therefore seem surprising that hard evidence on a comparative effectiveness of different selection techniques is not available, although some studies have been undertaken to compare results of the studies of each technique carried out separately. Closer consideration of the problem of measuring effectiveness helps, however, to reveal the difficulty of establishing valid results. In shortlisting or selecting a candidate it may, for example, be possible to review the extent to which the particular technique helped to predict successful performance of that candidate. It will, however, be highly unlikely to evaluate whether the rejected candidates would have been less, equally, or more able to perform than the selected candidate, because they were rejected and no opportunity was therefore afforded to evaluate their subsequent performance. There are very few true 'control' experiments in which suitable and unsuitable candidates are selected as a means of assessing the effectiveness of the selection technique. Consider further the difficulty of assessing the performance of the successful candidate. Failure to perform may be attributable to the candidate but equally it may be attributable to the way in which they were managed, the support provided, relationships with colleagues, the quality of the product on which they were working, or a host of other variables and it can rarely be the case that success or failure can be attributed wholly to the individual. Consider also the measures of success; is it the achievement of objectives or targets regardless of other aspects such as team relationships, or is it the quality of performance perhaps measured in team relationships or customer service, regardless of volume of output or targets achieved etc? Is success wholly a matter of performance, or does the length of time that the new person stays, or the amount of absence they incur, or their level of work satisfaction play any part in evaluating 'success'? In looking at the effectiveness of the selection technique, can it be assumed that the results of that technique contributed wholly, partly or not at all to the decision to select? Is a supervisor's rating a reliable indicator of successful performance?

The imponderables and variables outlined above are all reasons why care must be taken in accepting or rejecting the research into the effectiveness of any selection technique. Furthermore, when looking at the failure of techniques, consideration needs to be given as to whether the technique itself was inadequate or whether the way it was used rendered it ineffective.

Allowing for these considerations, it is still possible to gain a general view of the effectiveness of the various selection techniques. Taking a common scale from 0 to 1 one can undertake some guarded comparison. Zero reflects random choice, the toss of a coin. Choosing every sixth person to walk through the door would of course score 0 because as a random method it is no more effective than any other random choice. In so doing, however, it needs to be remembered that occasionally the sixth person through the door will be an effective performer purely by chance. Thus, selectors who believe in always choosing candidates with blue eyes, rejecting ones with white socks, or some other arbitrary factor will inevitably be able to point to examples of where 'their technique' brought measurable results. Perfect selection is measured as 1, that is to say the technique identifies the suitable candidate for the position every time. It is interesting to note that no technique has been proposed as, or been found to be, a perfect selection system. Good selection is therefore about improving the odds of success rather than guaranteeing it.

The *application form* has sometimes been reported as having a predictive validity (that is to say effective at predicting job performance or some other success factor) of 0.2. On the face of it, a fairly low predictive validity but care needs to be taken because much of the research has been on how they are used and what they measure rather than how well they measure. The low rating may therefore be more a reflection of the poor use of application forms than of the technique itself. Given the wide diversity of application forms it is also very difficult to achieve a standard assessment of them. Notable research by Herriot and Wingrove highlighted the idiosyncratic nature of assessors' evaluation of application forms where the likelihood of success by the candidate in securing an interview was attributed more to the amount of space taken up on the form than on the quality of the information contained within it, or any other significant factor. Notwithstanding the results of the studies, it must be true to say that, even allowing for occasional dishonesty, an application form must be an effective method (far greater than 0.2) of assessing whether an individual possesses certain academic qualifications, or professional certificates, or relevant experience and that, as long as it is used to screen for appropriate matters (ie acquired competencies), then it will be an effective technique, particularly if it is used properly with a clear rating or assessment system.

Various studies on *interview* effectiveness have demonstrated a significant difference between structured and unstructured interviews. Unstructured interviews generally have predictive validity of 0.2, with structured interviews averaging about 0.4 but with structured situational interviews scoring less, and structured behavioural interviews scoring more. Given that users of structured interviewing will usually have received training in such interviewing, there is the possibility that the heightened skill of the interviewer raises the results of the technique. Recent research has indicated that behavioural interviews (experienced-based) are more effective predictors of success than the situational (future scenario) interview, but that both benefit from certain aspects that improve their effectiveness; these include:

- proper job analysis to identify the key factors or competencies
- consistent and structured interview questions
- a panel of interviewers
- examples of effective questions
- a consistent rating system
- note-taking during the interview.

It has been concluded that, using this approach, the effectiveness of the interview is raised from 0.14 for traditional interviews to 0.56 for structured interviews, which makes it one of the most effective selection techniques.

One of the least researched aspects of selection is about the way in which the individual fits with the organisation culture or team. The limited research that has been undertaken indicates that the structured interview is one of the most effective ways of assessing the person–organisation fit.

The effectiveness of *psychometric tests* for predicting performance has been subject to a significant degree of research. It is, however, not without contention and results need to be treated carefully. The received wisdom is that ability and cognitive tests have a higher predictive validity than personality tests. Ability tests score at about 0.53, whereas personality tests score from 0.2 to 0.5 depending upon the research used.

Ability tests are fairly robust because the aspect they seek to assess, ie an observable or measurable skill, is easily measured and the test itself can therefore be validated. Designing a typing or spelling test or some other form of ability test is therefore, to a large extent, foolproof. The question 'why do ability tests not score more highly?' must therefore be raised, to which the answer is that the abilities that they measure are not always wholly or directly related to job performance. This is the case particularly where cognitive tests have been used to identify 'intelligence' for managerial posts but where no causal relationship has been shown to exist between intelligence and management performance. There are also some problems with test construction because many of the tests have been developed using schoolchildren or university students in the development stages but later applied to mature adults, and it is generally accepted that mental ability deteriorates with age. The additional benefits which the mature worker enjoys, however, around experience and decision-making for example, may allow 'wisdom' to more than compensate for any 'deficiencies' in mental ability and therefore enable them to give a higher performance than their youthful counterparts. Consequently, there may be doubts cast over the test, whereas it is the hypothesis which is unsound. Generally speaking, where an ability test is designed to measure an ability, and that ability is directly related to job performance, then the test will be an effective predictor.

Personality tests have been the subject of greater contention. One of the difficulties in establishing the effectiveness of personality tests is that research has been undertaken for many decades but until the last two decades or so there was no consensus on the components of personality. It was therefore difficult to conclude that they would predict anything if it wasn't known what they were trying to predict. For the last two decades there has been consensus on the 'big five' factors of personality and it has therefore become easier to research the effectiveness of personality tests in gauging personality and predicting work performance. Personality tests have a predictive validity of about 0.4. Behind this statement, however, lies a considerable degree of academic controversy. The prevailing view is that personality remains fairly constant over time. It is entirely feasible, therefore, that gauging personality accurately at a point in time will enable us to predict the broad patterns of behaviour etc which will be displayed by that person in subsequent life. Translating that prediction directly to work performance is, however, a huge leap. It may not necessarily be known whether the personality characteristic contributes positively or negatively to work performance, and there are difficulties in excluding consideration of the knowledge of the individual, or the fit with the environment, or the way in which they are managed. One of the difficulties of assessing the effectiveness of psychometric tests is the degree of contention which they provoke. Those who oppose them, often do so from a standpoint of ignorance or because they have been let down by placing too much reliance on a particular test. Those who promote their use can often do so with a conviction and enthusiasm which outstrips their validity. For certain positions, personality may be less important than other aspects such as acquired knowledge. It is therefore stretching the point to state that a psychometric test which properly predicts personality can be predictive of job performance, since such job performance may be attributable only in part to personality. In choosing a legal adviser, for example, greater importance would be attached to legal knowledge and qualifications than to personality characteristics. Conversely, selection of a sales representative in certain industries may not demand any prior knowledge or qualifications, and the personality characteristics which drive selling skills may be a more important – perhaps critical – selection criterion. Periodically in the UK there is a barrage of criticism vented against personality tests; such assaults are usually promulgated by one or two prominent individuals and generally coincide with publication of their new ability tests! Care needs to be taken, therefore, to assess the motive for such criticisms. While the research evidence on the predictive strengths of personality tests is interesting it is not always consistent. Invariably the results will also include the outcome of poorly-applied or unsuitable tests which will bring down the overall validity. More pertinent perhaps is that in practice very few organisations who use personality tests take the trouble to make generally available the information on their use and success. Many organisations that are satisfied with the use of the test and find it valuable in predicting job suitability of candidates, are not prepared to collect information on their success. There are many unpublished examples of the use of personality tests to identify predictors of job performance which are being used to improve the effectiveness of selection significantly.

Assessment centres generally have a very high predictive validity. This has to be a generalisation because assessment centres take many forms and there is difficulty in applying a common standard. It is nevertheless the case that assessment centres which comprise a range of selection techniques such as structured interviewing, testing, and exercises, will provide a higher validity than other techniques operated in isolation. There is, however, a need for a word of caution. Psychologists are very favourably inclined towards assessment centres and there is the danger that studies of their effectiveness may have been tainted with optimism. Of more concern, perhaps, are the criteria used to assess effectiveness. Two of the most commonly quoted are supervisor ratings of performance, and promotion success. It is of course the case that assessment centres are most frequently used for graduate selection or selection on to management development schemes. There is therefore a very strong possibility of self-fulfilling prophecies since promotion in most organisations with a graduate intake or management development scheme are given to those on such schemes. It is also the case that people on these schemes are rated by the person in charge of the graduate training scheme or management development programme who has an interest in seeing protégés succeed. Even where assessment is undertaken by the line-managers, they often take a lenient approach to rating because they know that a single poor assessment can 'damn' graduate trainees once and for all. It is also not unusual for eligibility to attend assessment centres to be restricted by certain criteria; for internal centres this may be a supervisor's pre-assessment, for external centres it may be a degree qualification. Where there is pre-selection, the possibility cannot be ruled out that all candidates would have been suitable. Notwithstanding these caveats, the assessment centre is almost certainly the most effective selection technique.

Although *biodata* is not extensively used in selection in the UK, it has an extensive body of research to provide an insight into its effectiveness. Most of the research has been undertaken in the USA but research undertaken in the UK has mirrored the findings of US research and serve to demonstrate that cultural differences will not distort the research findings.

Biodata has been impressively validated in predicting a number of work-related factors including performance, absenteeism, job tenure, and income. The most frequently quoted review has not been an academic study but a practical study of biodata in use in Standard Oil of Indiana in the 1960s. Biodata was administered to a group of petroleum research scientists and validated and cross-validated against three different criteria of overall performance ratings, creativity ratings, and number of patents. The validation for the criteria were 0.61, 0.52 and 0.52 respectively, which provides a very significant degree of correlation. In the 1980s a flurry of large-scale research projects and meta-analysis of other studies consistently demonstrated the effectiveness of biodata as a predictor of performance and other work-related aspects. The studies varied in their rating of biodata from 0.34 to 0.46. Many of the researchers have placed a high value on the predictive validity of biodata, in some cases running second only to assessment centres and in some cases slightly less than ability tests. In addition to predicting performance, however, biodata has been seen to be very effective as an indicator of potential absenteeism and retention.

Different assessment methods will not always yield exactly the same results, but they will tend to point recruiters in the same direction. Table 6 overleaf gives an interesting example of the candidate profiles produced for a single individual through structured interview and psychological testing.

Acceptability

In addition to consideration of the suitability of the technique for the aspects being measured, the effectiveness of the technique in measuring such aspects, and the resource and cost considerations to apply it, consideration also needs to be given to the acceptability of the technique. Acceptability may be looked at in a number of ways:

- client acceptability
- candidate acceptability
- ethical and legal acceptability.

Acceptability to clients is an important point because, for example, a line manager who does not endorse the use of psychometric testing will dismiss it as a 'black box' and disregard any information, however valuable, that flows from it. It is of course, not only the client but sometimes the selector who may be sceptical of a particular technique; it is often the case that biodata scores are at odds with interviewers' perceptions

Table 6
CANDIDATE PROFILE COMPARISONS

The reports below are real results relating to the same person. They are two extracts taken from interview and psychometric testing. Both were undertaken independently of each other or any other technique.

Report from a structured interview	Feedback from psychometric test
Confidently infer a strong ability at both the implementation and strategic level . . .	. . . thinks ahead, organises, plans, and makes a systematic effort to reach objectives on schedule.
Leaves me in no doubt he can take people with him . . .	Responds to opportunities for taking the lead and being given responsibility but may be resistant to too much direction from others.
An individual able to see what a given problem is and then select one or two of the major options for resolving and to drive through to good effect.	. . . stimulated by problems where he can find and implement new solutions . . . run the risk of deciding too quickly before firstly examining the situation.
. . . works as a team player . . .	. . . will enjoy demonstrating being part of a group.

and can cause some difficulty if used as a shortlisting technique. Given that biodata can be a more effective predictor than certain kinds of interview an interesting conflict arises as to which technique should be given the greater credence. In practice, acceptability will usually win over effectiveness, which underlines the importance of this aspect in choosing techniques. There is no comprehensive research into the reasons behind discomfort with certain techniques, but in general it may be said that:

- interviews can feel uncomfortable with interviewers being more conscious of their own performance in the interview than that of the interviewee and an awkwardness of knowing what questions to ask and how to gauge the suitability of answers given. Structured interviews overcome these problems, but then create others, such as the interviewer feeling awkward in coming to terms with the structure of a controlled process and so avoiding structured questions, while delivery becoming staccato rather than a fluid dialogue of investigation.

- biodata creates discomfort because it cannot provide substantiated reasons for its conclusions and is therefore difficult to grasp. It is seen as a black box and its results often differ from interview ratings.

- ability tests, and particularly the way in which they are administered, create discomfort in treating candidates as schoolchildren rather than adults, while personality tests are sometimes seen as rather vague and meaningless questions which cannot be relied upon to support the conclusions drawn. Sometimes the reports from personality tests are as impenetrable as the tests themselves and are peppered with 'psycho-babble' that leaves line managers unimpressed. Tests which use bar chart profiles and other diagrammatic devices to present the data are more popular with clients.

- assessment centres can be seen as tedious, time-consuming, and often overly academic and impractical, with many line managers attributing a low validity which is at great odds with the published data.

These are, of course, generalisations and they are not universal beliefs. There are many interviewers who praise biodata, many line managers with an evangelical zeal for psychometric testing, and senior executives who place great reliance upon the outcome of assessment centres. Acceptability of selection methods to clients is like the acceptability of anything else – one person's meat is another person's poison. Some investigations have been undertaken into client preferences for selection techniques. In the USA in 1996, executives were asked to rate various selection methods according to their perceived effectiveness for identifying high-performing employees. It should be noted that this was not a wholly subjective process and that many of the organisations relied upon internal studies of the validation of the various techniques. The results were rated on a scale of 1 for 'no good' through 3 for 'average' to 5 for 'extremely good'. The results were:

work samples	3.68
references or recommendation	3.49
unstructured interviews	3.49
structured interviews	3.42
assessment centres	3.42
specific aptitude tests	3.08
personality tests	2.93
cognitive ability tests	2.89
biodata	2.84

A study in the UK of small businesses (one-third of the UK workforce is employed by the 88 per cent of businesses that employ fewer than 25 people) showed that 92 per cent used formal interviews (of which 66 per cent used unstructured interviews and 34 per cent used structured interviews), 44 per cent used work trials or realistic work previews for a week or so, 18 per cent used job simulations, 18 per cent used literacy and numeracy tests, 15 per cent used ability tests and 3.6 per cent used personality tests. Fewer than 20 per cent used a formal application form in order to gather information on candidates, 27 per cent using a CV and 20 per cent relying on general letters; but 58 per cent used face-to-face interviews to gather the data and 20 per cent obtained it over the telephone. In terms of usefulness, the interview was deemed to be the most useful method, with references, CVs and application forms some way behind, and work trials, ability and personality tests as the least useful.

In a survey of 160 UK organisations undertaken by Industrial Relations Services and published in 1987, the most frequently employed selection methods were interviews, used by almost 100 per cent of the organisations, (over 72 per cent using structured interviews), 76 per cent using ability and aptitude tests, 61 per cent using personality questionnaires, 50 per cent using literacy and numeracy tests, and 45 per cent using assessment centres. Screening was undertaken mainly by application forms, used by 94 per cent, and CVs 76 per cent. Telephone screening was used by only 24 per cent (but this represented a significant growth from the previous research some five years earlier) with only 5 per cent using biodata. This represents the general response but the survey also provided information on the way in which certain techniques are more or less prevalent for the selection of certain occupational groups.

The respondents were also asked to nominate the best selection methods, which again differed between occupational groups but overall came out as follows:

interviews	68.9%
application forms	11.1%
CVs	8.5%
assessment centres	7.6%
ability and aptitude tests	2.3%

Nearly all employers used references but this was an area of concern since many were more inclined to ask for references than to provide them, and many were wary of the reliance that could be placed upon references given. Just over half of the respondents requested references before offering a job but the survey did not indicate how many took up references before making their selection decision.

One of the interesting facets of the IRS survey is that it highlights the contrasting views of academics and practitioners. Until the last decade, academics dismissed interviews as little better than chance selection and, even now, regard only structured interviews as having any degree of (limited) effectiveness. Yet practitioners cited the interview as being not only a very common technique but also a very useful one. Academics have a high regard for ability tests but such regard is not shared by practitioners and furthermore the IRS survey would suggest that where literacy, numeracy and some other ability tests are used, their purpose is more of an 'excuse' to reduce unwanted volumes of applications. It is also noteworthy that the great body of academic research among psychologists confirms the big five factor theory of personality and that efforts to replicate the findings of Cattell's 16 factors of personality have not been successful, nor have efforts to justify greater numbers of factors such as the 32 used in the Occupational Personality Questionnaire. Similarly, instruments such as Belbin's team roles or the Myers-Briggs® Indicator have not been corroborated by independent research and, although useful for development purposes, are not regarded as having any reliance for selection purposes, while the Personal Profile Analysis (hitherto known as the Thomas International or Disc) is not without significant concern over its validity. In the IRS survey, the most popular proprietary selection tests were the OPQ, 16PF, the Personal Profile Analysis, Belbin, FIRO-B, the Myers Briggs® Type Indicator, and the Perception and Preference Inventory, none of which adhere to the established principle of the big five factors of personality or enjoy widespread academic support. Similarly, biodata, which has very high predictive validity and is popular with academics, is not so popular with practitioners.

It may be the case, therefore, that rationality is not a prime determinant in favouring selection techniques but that ease of use, understanding and the presentation of data are more important considerations than effectiveness or cost. It is also the case, of course, that the most popular tests in use are those which are marketed most effectively and it may be that selectors respond to the sales overtures of test publishers rather than deciding on the need for a test and then undertaking a survey of available choices. Finally, the influence of fashion should not be ruled out, and in choosing techniques, recruiters may be more influenced by those in use in other organisations and their 'track record' than deciding to embark on protracted investigations into the efficiency of the techniques or products. Certainly practical considerations alone would not explain the differences in the popularity of techniques differing between countries. One study of selection techniques in French and British firms gave the following comparisons of usage:

assessment centres used in	18.8% of French firms	58.9% of British firms
biodata used in	3.8% of French firms	19.1% of British firms
personality tests used in	17.0% of French firms	9.6% of British firms
graphology used in	77.0% of French firms	0.0% of British firms

There is little reason to suspect that practitioners in either country are less concerned with issues of effectiveness, usability and cost.

Acceptability to candidates of selection techniques has not been greatly researched. There has been some academic research including research into the impact on morale and performance, but it has generally been contradictory. Research by practitioners is similarly uncommon although some organisations take time to canvass the views of both successful and unsuccessful applicants and candidates to gauge their perceptions of the process, their feelings about the company, and concerns about fairness (particularly equality of opportunity).

The degree of familiarity will, of course, influence perceptions of the process; while candidates may be irritated by the need to complete an application form, particularly if it is poorly designed, they are unlikely to condemn it as inappropriate or intrusive since they will expect it to be part of the standard selection process. Allowing for differences in the results of the various forms of research, the perceptions of candidates seem to be as follows:

- Application forms are generally an expected and uneventful part of the selection process and are taken in their stride by most candidates. They are resented most at senior levels where candidates prefer to prepare their own CV (and can be particularly irritated if asked to complete one after a CV has already been provided), and they are intimidating for manual workers unaccustomed to completion of 'official forms'.

- Interviews are similarly regarded as an expected part of the process and the lack of interview is regarded more unfavourably than 'failure' at interview. It is the case, however, that candidates' perceptions are more strongly influenced by the *conduct* of the interview than by the interview itself, and a badly handled interview is more damaging than no interview at all. There seems to be no evidence that panel interviews are regarded as any more intimidating to candidates than one-to-one interviews, and structured interviews are not seen as being any more demanding by candidates than unstructured interviews. The structured situational interview is, however, regarded as a hurdle by some candidates, particularly for manual workers where the ambiguity of non-specific future situations and the need to describe hypothetical responses in an abstract language contrast sharply with the specificity of real circumstances and the limited 'earthy' language in everyday use. The behavioural-based or experience-based structured interview does not suffer from such a drawback and although it may appear to be an interrogation from the interviewer's perspective, feedback from candidates indicates that they are more at ease with the process and consider it to be wholly relevant to the selection procedure.

- Biodata has had a mixed review, with some studies showing that candidates perceived it to be less invasive than ability tests and other techniques, while some showed that there was candidate hostility to the process. In some cases biodata has ceased to be used because of hostility from candidates, and although its use is most frequent with graduates there is some evidence that even graduates find it unwelcome. It tends to be most acceptable when included as a supplementary part of an orthodox application form.

- Ability tests have a mixed reception. Graduates and school-leavers accustomed to examinations and tests rarely resent them but some groups find them deeply offensive. Ability tests are proven to be more difficult for older workers, and since test norms are usually developed with graduates and schoolchildren they may be viewed as unduly hard and be resented by old workers. Candidates for managerial and professional roles can be puzzled by 'school tests' which bear little relation to the realities of their roles; and ethnic groups, against whom they may be discriminatory, can be offended by their use, particularly where the tests are for abilities which bear no relation to the qualities needed for the position being filled. It is probable that more legal actions have been taken against employers over the use of ability tests than over any other technique.

- Assessment centres are generally well received and, if properly handled, can even be enjoyed by candidates. There is clear evidence that where feedback is provided to candidates (a frequent feature of assessment centres) the candidate's perception of the selection process is very favourable, regardless of success or failure.

Given the lack of hard evidence of candidates' perceptions of the selection process, it is important that organisations under-take periodic surveys of candidates' reactions to the selection process. This should be the case particularly where the selection is undertaken by a third party, such as a recruitment agency on behalf of the organisation, since it is not uncommon for administrative convenience and economic considerations to outweigh considerations of courtesy to candidates; it is regrettably not uncommon for some agencies to fail to acknowledge receipt of applications or to advise on the outcome. It is not uncommon for agencies to write to candidates 'should you not hear from us in the next x weeks you should presume that . . .' etc. Disaffected candidates can all too easily become disenchanted customers. In the USA, for example, it has been estimated that one in four of the working population has either worked for, or applied for, employment with McDonalds; the potential impact upon the business of the way such candidates are treated is very clear, and provides sound commercial reasons for handling them well.

Ethical and legal considerations are important because there are many opportunities for unfair discrimination to creep into the selection process, from the development of a person-specification based on stereotypes of race or sex or physical ability, through to prejudices in decision-making. There is, however, also the opportunity for direct and indirect discrimination to creep into the selection process through the choice of technique.

Application forms and biodata are not in themselves dis-criminatory except in the case of people with sight difficulties and where there is insistence upon the application being completed in 'your own handwriting'. (How can applicants complete in someone else's handwriting?) Discrimination can, however, creep into the components of the application form or into the questions within the biodata. Questions on the application form about marital status could, for example, be held to be an intention to discriminate, as can asking questions about sex and race, which is why many recruiters now use a separate section to gather this information for equal opportunities monitoring, and which can therefore clearly be seen to play no part in the decision-making process. Great care needs to be taken in the design of biodata to avoid it becoming a

discriminatory instrument, particularly since it uses the principle of coincidences and may therefore perpetuate a workforce which is not truly balanced in terms of sex and race etc.
Generally speaking, however, both biodata and application
forms can be carefully designed to ensure they become an
objective part of the assessment process which promotes
equality of opportunity.

The interview is the most frequently used selection technique in the UK. There is evidence – both from research and
legal cases – that discriminatory decisions can be made from
the interview and, of course, prejudices of the interviewer will
directly impact on whether the process is discriminatory or
not. These, however, are aspects of how the interview is used
rather than the interview itself. Is the technique itself discriminatory? The answer seems to be 'perhaps'. An investigation by the Commission for Racial Equality in 1984 looked at
a Leicester engineering company and concluded that Afro-
Caribbean and Asian candidates had been unsuccessful either
because of an inability to communicate or an inability to
answer interview questions to the panel's satisfaction. Other
ethnic candidates were unsuccessful for other reasons, but
such reasons were consistent with reasons given for the failure of white candidates; however, none of the white candidates suffered because of the communication difficulty. The
investigation also looked at the interview structure that used
a situational interview which asks people to think ahead to a
hypothetical future situation and answer how they would
respond to it. It was concluded that ethnic minority applicants, with less likelihood to have English as their first language, would suffer unfairly by being hampered in inferring
the panel's intentions from the language used to phrase the
questions, and being able to frame a response in a similar way.
It was also found that the vocabulary and tone of answers
from Asian candidates made it more difficult for the interviewers to evaluate the response. There is a further concern,
which is that in many cases the interview is used to measure
the person-organisation fit. The likelihood of an ethnic minority candidate 'fitting' a predominantly white workforce, or of
a female candidate 'fitting' a predominantly male workforce,
or a physically disabled candidate 'fitting' a sports-oriented

workforce is the rationalisation of prejudice. The unstructured interview of course has the potential to be more discriminatory, particularly where the questions are loosely and thoughtlessly phrased. Even where the answers are not taken into consideration for decision-making, such questions as 'When do you intend to start a family?' or 'Can you wear a hard hat on your turban?' may, not surprisingly, lead the candidate to believe that they are likely to be discriminated against. Notes taken in unstructured interviews can reveal unconscious discrimination, as in the Commission for Racial Equality investigation into the recruitment of chartered accountant trainees in 1987.

Psychometric testing has not been without its challenges for discrimination. Generally speaking, most proprietary personality tests have been carefully designed to ensure that the questions they ask are not discriminatory and that the scoring mechanism does not disadvantage racial or sex types. Ability tests have, however, probably been a greater source of discrimination cases than any other selection technique. Well-publicised cases in the UK against British Rail and London Underground, although being settled before being heard in court, have focused much attention on such parts of the selection process. In broad terms, an ability test which discriminates against a protected group but which properly tests an appropriate indicator of performance will not be held to be unfairly discriminatory. In the UK there is currently no discrimination law concerning age, which is as well because most ability tests measure skills that deteriorate with age. That in itself may not be alarming, but the standards for the tests are usually set by university students or schoolchildren rather than by real performers in the workplace. The primary reason, however, for actions against ability tests is the careless selection of the tests. Tests of verbal prowess will obviously discriminate against those whose first language is not English and to use them for the selection of manual roles where language is unimportant is at best a waste of money. The widespread use of literacy and numeracy tests without full consideration of their relevance and purpose is perhaps the most worrying aspect of the use of ability tests.

The key element in ensuring ethical and legal acceptability

of any selection technique is to ensure that the criteria which have been set for selection are free from bias and are wholly relevant to the performance of the role, that all candidates are treated in a consistent way, that redundant items are excluded from the application form, interview, structure etc, that questions on application forms and in interviews are carefully framed around the key competencies and phrased in a non-discriminatory way (and interpreted and scored accordingly), that tests are used only where they measure aspects pertinent to the role, and the performance of the techniques are monitored for equal opportunities to ensure that they do not discriminate unfairly on sex, race or disability. There is no legal barrier to discrimination on grounds of religion in Great Britain or on grounds of sexual orientation or age in the UK, but an ethical approach will ensure that similar consideration is given to these aspects.

Deciding on selection techniques

It can be seen that the decision on which technique to use to support selection decisions is one requiring a balanced judgement. It may be feasible to develop a score-card to assist in the selection by adding weight to each of the factors. There is, however, a danger in becoming overly rigid and mechanistic in such an approach and it may be better simply to keep the four decision points in mind when making a final choice. There are, however, three key preliminaries which need to be addressed in order to make an effective choice. These are:

- the selection ratio for the positions to be filled. This is the likelihood of people being able to do the job. A selection ratio of 0.5 means there is a fifty/fifty chance of people being able to perform the job if picked at random, 1 means that anybody picked would be able to do the job and 0.1 means that only one in 10 people selected at random for the job would be able to it. This is merely applying a statistical device to the common-sense notion that some simple jobs can be done by most people whereas fewer people would be available to perform more complex jobs. This may seem an obvious point but all too often decisions are made to apply expensive selection techniques to fairly straightforward selection.

- the interplay of techniques. This is important and it has been shown that where all parts of the selection process contribute to the final decision, often building up as independent pieces of the jigsaw, the success rate is much greater than where each of the techniques is used as a hurdle to screen out for the next part of the selection process and is then ignored once that latter part is underway. This is a significant point because it is all too often the practice that application forms and the information on them are ignored once later stages, such as the interview or testing, are under way and they do not feature in the final decision-making. The selection will be more efficient if all parts of the process are combined and reviewed at the final selection decision point.

- that there is a clear idea of the criteria for selection, preferably in the form of defined competencies. This is the most important prerequisite. The development of a clear specification is set out in Chapters 5 and 6; without such clarity it is difficult to identify which techniques are the most useful for assessing the various criteria, and although the techniques are all to varying degrees efficient at removing the hay from the haystack, they cannot in themselves paint the picture of the needle.

With these three pre-requisites in mind, it is then possible to proceed with considerations of the suitability of the techniques for assessing the criteria, keeping in mind the relative importance of natural, acquired, adapting and performing competencies. It is possible to consider the resource cost constraints, predict the acceptability to clients, to candidates and the ethical and legal considerations, and to consider the effectiveness of each technique bearing in mind, of course, that the more difficult the selection ratio the more weight will be attached to the effectiveness of the technique.

PART 3

TECHNIQUES

8

ATTRACTING APPLICANTS

'Marketing' employment

There are some essential costs involved in selecting people. There can be the hidden costs of time and effort involved in sifting through the information on the new person contained in their CV checking up on their references and preparing for the interview, etc. There may be more visible costs of time spent interviewing the successful candidate, perhaps the cost of test materials or other ancillaries, perhaps the cost of relocating the new person. There will also be the cost of bringing the new person up to speed in terms of training and development. All of these, and other costs related to the successful candidate, are necessary investments in securing an effective new employee. All other costs are unnecessary; they are incidental to the process. The costs of dealing with unwanted applications, of interviewing unsuccessful candidates, of advertisements the successful candidate did not see, correspondence with unsuccessful candidates, etc are all non-productive. They do not contribute to the successful integration or acquisition of the new person and are therefore unnecessary. Unnecessary is not, however, always unavoidable. Cost-effective selection is concerned with avoiding unnecessary costs, albeit recognising a realistic target will be to minimise rather than eliminate unnecessary costs. One of the most effective ways to minimise unnecessary costs and raise the standard of response is an effective approach to marketing the 'employment product'.

Selection is, of course, a two-way process; it is about matching people and roles. Selectors know a great deal about the jobs but are disadvantaged in trying to gauge and gather information on the candidate. The candidate knows, usually, all about himself or herself but is disadvantaged in trying to gauge and gather information about the job. Good selectors therefore ensure that there is a high degree of self-selection in the overall process, that is to say the candidates are given plenty of information to help them select in or out of the over-all process. This process begins with the marketing strategy for employment in the organisation.

There is a view that selectors are buyers; candidates are sell-ers in that they sell their labour and will continue to be sell-ers of their labour for so long as the organisation requires. In practice it is more effective if selectors see themselves as sell-ers rather than buyers; to be the agents of an investment com-pany in which people continue to invest their time and effort. By taking the perspective of sellers it is possible to think about 'selling' employment and focus attention on how to market those jobs to aid the selling process. Adopting the marketing approach is a very effective means of minimising unnecessary costs and improving the quality of candidates by attracting the right buyer. The classic approach to the mar-keting of products is concerned with:

- research
- planning
- positioning
- supporting.

The development of an employment marketing strategy can benefit from adopting the same approach.

Market research

Product market research is concerned with identifying con-sumer needs, and covers five main types of research:

- market research – who buys in what quantity?
- product research – what is right and wrong with the prod-ucts of the company?
- marketing method research – are we communicating and distributing effectively?

- motivational research – why do people buy the products they do and what do they feel about them?
- attitude surveys – customers' attitudes to the products and the companies that make them.

In this sense the 'market' is concerned with the potential source of labour, the types of people who 'buy in' to the company.

The 'product' is concerned with the jobs on offer, their nature, their suitability and attractiveness to people. It is concerned with the good and bad points of working for the organisation and the particular type of work that is being undertaken.

In the same way that marketers would pay attention to the marketing method research to check that the method of communication, the message, and the reach are effective, so too do recruiters need to be concerned that cost-effective channels are being used to get the message across.

In product marketing, attention is paid to motivational research to identify the 'emotional purchase' of consumers. It is interesting that in 'marketing' employment, greater attention seems to be paid to winning minds rather than hearts and a greater emphasis on logic than feelings. It is particularly interesting, given that research on labour turnover shows that a very small percentage of people leave organisations for logical reasons, that the greatest influence is emotive reasons. Greater attention to assessing the motivation of existing and potential employees and a greater emphasis on selling to the heart as much as to the mind will increase the cost-effectiveness of recruitment marketing.

Attitude surveys present an interesting perspective for the recruiter. It is usual to find industrial relations staff taking responsibility for employee attitude surveys – or perhaps pay designers or organisation development staff. There is a view that recruiters bring the people in to the organisation and that their work ends there. Yet effective recruitment is one that leads to a long-term mutually beneficial relationship between employee and employer. In product marketing it is not unusual for marketers to concentrate effort on reminding existing consumers of the benefits of their purchase in order to retain brand loyalty. It is not unwise for organisations to continue to remind employees of the value of their 'purchase' in buying in to the company. It is not unrealistic for recruiters to take responsibility for the on-going assessment of internal attitudes and the on-going promotion of the benefits of the 'purchase'.

Planning

The five stages of planning product marketing can be effectively applied to employment marketing. Each stage will be considered in turn.

Formulate overall direction and goal

In product terms this is identifying the business that a company is in and the market in which it seeks to operate. In employment marketing terms this stage should be identifying the labour market in which the organisation is going to compete.

Identifying the external opportunities

A parallel in employment marketing is to consider the potential for sources of labour in the same way that product marketers would look at the potential for selling their product. Using the seller's perspective it is identifying which groups of people are likely to want to buy into employment with the company.

Identifying the external threats

In product marketing this is to identify the threats, whether from competition, demand or other social factors. In the employment marketing perspective this is concerned with identifying other recruiters of, and therefore competitors for, external labour. This may seem an obvious point, but all too often organisations compare themselves with others pursuing the same nature of business when in reality they may be geographically remote and not true competitors for labour – whereas other quite dissimilar organisations in the locality may be strongly competing for the same labour. This stage extends beyond looking simply at competitors and will also be concerned with legislative or other impacts that may pose a threat. Changing demographics, whether the baby boom or pensioner boom, will be an obvious aspect for consideration.

Produce the marketing objectives and strategy

This is a key aspect in product marketing, but in employment marketing terms it is an aspect which is often overlooked. All too often recruiters are attempting to use clever advertising techniques or throw additional money at recruiting people once in 'the eye of the storm' rather than looking ahead to identify the oncoming problem and putting strategies in place to prevent the problem or minimise the adverse consequences. This, of course, will be more critical for in-house recruiters with long-term perspectives, than external consultants who may be undertaking a one-off assignment.

Programming the marketing mix to support the product

In product marketing, the marketing mix is looking at:

- the product elements
- the pricing elements
- the promotion elements.

In employment terms this will be an activity beyond the scope of the recruiter alone and will be an aspect which demands the attention of a range of human resources management. It is, however, something with which the recruiters must be involved. For the 'product elements' we can read the nature and scope of roles and the structure of the organisation. Since recruiters are attuned to the expectation of people in the external labour market they should have a valid contribution to make in the shaping of the organisation structure – the careers and opportunities that will exist for people in addition to the way in which roles are designed to make use of the talent available and thereby improve the intrinsic value and attractiveness of such employment. For the 'pricing elements' we can read levels of salary and reward. This is usually the domain of the compensation and benefits people within the organisation and may be the product of collective bargaining arrangements. Since the primary purpose of any pay structure

is likely to be concerned with either the recruitment or retention of staff, and since one of the big influences in attracting
people to the organisation will be the price tag on their services, it seems obvious that recruiters need to input into
reward decisions. The 'promotion elements' cover aspects
such as advertising, public relations, direct and indirect promotion. The promotion elements need to be forward looking.
It is unlikely that product marketing nowadays will rely solely
on advertising but will look at a complete range of strategies.
So, too, must employment marketing. This is further discussed in 'Supporting' below.

Positioning

In product marketing terms, positioning is concerned with
setting the image of the product and identifying the target
consumer audience. It is, of course, concerned with the
product itself and the stage in the life cycle of the product.
Consumer products are seen as having life cycles through
which they progress:

- introduction
- growth
- maturity
- decline
- phase out.

Marketers are conscious of the phase 'in the life cycle of the
product' in determining the degree of support and positioning
given to the product. In employment terms this is an unusual
aspect since for many years recruiters have been focused on
bringing in people for long-term contracts with the organisation, very often for life-time careers. In recent years the nature
of employment has changed dramatically and the paradigms
have shifted significantly. It is now the case in many organisations that there may be a group of core employees with permanent 'career' prospects, and other groups of peripheral
employees, some of whom will be on short-term contracts,
others on part-time, freelance or contract arrangements. In
the organisation there may be some roles where there is a
shortage of skills and a perceived long-term growth, perhaps

in technology or other aspects. In other parts of the organisation there may be a phasing out of certain roles as technology, new developments or market changes affect the demand for such labour. It is naive to believe that labour is so flexible that people can be shifted from the phased-out jobs into the growth jobs. Careful thought needs to be given, therefore, to the marketing of the various kinds of employment. Organisations have suffered severe problems in recent years where employees recruited into roles in the 'decline' or 'phase out' employment life-cycle, have been recruited on the promise (sometimes explicit, sometimes implied) of long-term careers. In today's employment market it is essential to look at the life cycle of the employment product and to position it accordingly. It is also important that the employment product should be given a brand strategy for maximum marketing impact. There are many successful examples of marketing strategies for products. One of the most successful and enduring has been that of BMW, the car maker. BMW has created a successful product image and its familiar blue and white round logo is instantly recognisable by a large target audience and is identified with the key brand aspects which the company aims to portray, such as prestige, innovation, build-quality and safety. Within the overall brand image, however, each of the products has its own positioning. The luxury cars under the 'Series 7' banner are positioned at financially successful, older groups and stress luxury and prestige as key selling points. The '5 Series' is positioned for the family executive who needs a car large enough to house a mature family but who still has some of the prestige aspirations of the 7 series. The '3 Series' is targeted at the aspiring executive, perhaps with a young family, and is positioned as a rung on the ladder of the luxury brand. The features it promotes are concerned with performance and handling rather than sophisticated luxury. Each of the brands has its own distinct entity and its own target audience and yet it is encompassed within an overall brand image which is mutually supportive and which ensures that none of the individual brands detracts from the others but is part of a supportive whole. Given that many organisations in today's world encompass a range of different employment prospects within a single organisation, there is much to be gained by learning from the successful approach taken by organisations such as BMW to their product marketing.

Supporting

Once the research planning and positioning has been undertaken it is possible to move on to the targeted support for marketing employment in the organisation. There will be a very clear understanding and agreement on the positioning of the employment package in its various forms, the intrinsic (motivational) and extrinsic (salary and reward) features of the package, and a clear understanding, through the research, of the attractiveness of employment with the organisation. The expectations, competitive pressures etc, will combine to give a clear focus to the work needed. This will also enable decisions to be made on the most appropriate support for marketing the product. In the same way that the product marketers would look at the appropriate medium for communicating their message to the target audience so too will the target audience or labour market and its preferences dictate the approach taken to supporting employment marketing. It is not therefore simply a matter of advertising but of considering the various approaches that will be available to the recruiter. These may include:

- public relations
- in-house promotions
- direct mail
- advertising.

Public relations

It is not generally thought that recruiters should play a pivotal role in the public relations of an organisation. In general, public relations is handled by specialists either in-house in the case of large organisations or by using external consultants in the smaller organisations. In the private sector the focus, particularly for share-quoted companies, is on the message to investors. In the public sector, if public relations is undertaken, it is usually to ensure an appreciation among the 'consumers' of the value of the service being received. It is very rare that public relations specialists consider the impact of a public relations effort on existing employees, let alone on potential employees. It remains the case, however, that most potential employees gain more of a 'feel' for the organisation through its public relations effort or product marketing endeavours than through the influence of the HR department. It is important, therefore, that recruiters use the opportunity to influence the formal public relations or product marketing strategies of the organisation by indicating the messages that they would wish to convey to the audience to whom they wish to communicate. There are numerous occasions where organisations have lampooned themselves and their staff in an effort to project humour into their product marketing, only to find an adverse reaction from potential employees (and sometimes also from existing employees). In addition to the formal public relations effort, there are many activities that the recruiters can undertake directly, or influence others to undertake with them. Local trade shows, career fairs, liaison with schools and universities and appearances at local associations from Chambers of Commerce to Women's Institutes (depending, of course, on the target audience and the labour market) are all effective. These are, however, time-consuming activities and need money to be spent if they are to be undertaken professionally. It is also essential that they are undertaken on a planned and regular basis. In recent years, for example, blue chip companies have differed in their approach to the graduate recruitment market. Some companies have chosen to scale down their drives but to continue them regularly. Others have chosen to adopt a stop-start approach, continuing high visibility in some years and withdrawing completely in others. In the case of the stop-start approach, the absence speaks as loudly *against* the company in the 'stop' times as the promotional efforts speaks *for* the company in the 'start' times.

In-house promotion

Many organisations are involved in providing a product or a service to members of the public, or perhaps among the groups in their target audience or labour market. In such cases it can be very effective to promote the prospect of employment opportunities through this medium. This is nothing new; for many years the local shop has advertised for staff by simply putting a sign in its window. Given that recruiters need to avoid unnecessary work and expenditure, it is important to ensure that this promotion provides a sufficiently good picture to attract suitable candidates and deter unsuitable candidates. Some organisations have sufficient space to be able to site a permanent display stand with available information and application forms. Other organisations find it possible to incorporate publicity on careers in their general product or service catalogues. In general, in-house promotion is most often used for lower-level general staff but, curiously, there are many occasions when organisations looking for scarce specialist skills fail to promote their career opportunities in sales and other material to their customers, even when the customers are the very specialists the organisation is trying so hard to attract.

Direct mail

The age of 'junk mail' is a regret to many. It is, however, a modern phenomenon and it tends to be a source only of anger or resentment when it is persistent or intrusive and where its product or service is unwanted. In general, it is only junk when people don't want the product; otherwise it is an effective means of selling, and those who have bought a wanted item through such a process are not resentful of it. It is also the case that mail which asks the recipient to give something is far less welcome than mail which offers to give something to the recipient. In such terms the interest in direct mail to advertise employment is likely to be more cordial than most direct mail aimed at stimulating a purchase. The quality of focus offered by direct mail is unparalleled. It is possible to obtain information on names and addresses categorised in various ways, whether it be social, economic, consumer habits, political persuasion, or financial standing, etc. Good market research will provide information on the target audience for employment which can be matched very precisely to the direct mail campaign. This can be undertaken either in-house by buying-in appropriate mail lists, or by specialist organisations that can arrange the appropriate level of service. This may be something as simple as stuffing and posting envelopes, through to a total campaign in which letters are prepared individually and personalised using a computer database and mail-merge facilities, posted, followed up with telephone calls and tracked. The use of the Post Office 'mailsort' facility enables large-scale mailings to be pre-sorted (by postcode) by the organisation in order to achieve substantial cost savings on postage.

Advertising

Advertising tends to be the most popular communication channel for recruiters. It can take a number of forms, including:

- static: newspaper, magazine or periodical advertising and job centres
- live: radio, cinema and television advertising
- interactive: internet advertising, recruitment fairs or events.

Static advertising

This may perhaps be in national or local newspapers. Nowadays many local newspapers are supplemented by free newspapers which derive income from advertisers rather than from readers. The use of the newspaper will depend upon the kind of post to be filled and the target audience. National newspapers generally carry advertisements for more senior positions and, although they are able to advertise each day, generally give prominence to different types of advertising on different days. It is often the case that job advertisements are carried on a Thursday or a Sunday. The advantage of national newspapers is that they are published more frequently and it is possible to place an advertisement at relatively short notice. The advertisements need to be correctly prepared, which usually means using a specialist advertising agency, and the national newspapers tend to be the most expensive form of advertising, costing several thousand pounds. Local newspapers are usually much cheaper, although those serving large areas such as London will be on a par with the cost of national advertising. Where employment is targeted at a specific group, perhaps engineers, IT people or HR staff etc, but where the target audience is scattered over a wide geographical area – perhaps nationally – the use of specialist periodicals and trade journals is often the preferred approach. It is usually (but not always) the case that the specialist journals are far cheaper than national newspaper advertising, but more expensive than local newspaper advertising. The benefit of using such media is that it is targeted directly at the appropriate group and therefore minimises response from unsuitable candidates. The downside is that such journals may appear on a monthly basis and it is several weeks before an advertisement can be placed, which causes an unwelcome delay in the selection process.

Live advertising

Radio and television advertising is usually the domain of product advertising. Television advertising for employment is very rare and is usually seen only for large recruiters, such as the Army. The cost of preparing and screening a television advertisement is on a par with the whole HR budget for many organisations. It also takes a significant time to prepare an advertisement and the fees for peak slots are more expensive and generally less often available at short notice. All of these aspects conspire to make television advertising generally unsuitable. A lower cost option suitable for a younger general target audience, and where time is not a problem (for example, pre-planned graduate intakes), is cinema advertising which can be very effective. It also offers the opportunity to localise the advertisement.

Radio advertising is generally much cheaper to prepare than television and cinema advertising, is generally cheaper to broadcast, and carries fewer problems of availability or lead times. It can be a very effective means of advertising, although it is more difficult to target particular audiences. It can be particularly effective when used to reinforce other advertising, for example by prompting people to read a newspaper advertisement on a particular evening or to visit an open evening at a particular location. One of the advantages of using live advertising is that it has a very wide coverage, usually far greater than those reading newspapers, and gains attention in ways that the other media cannot. For example, newspaper advertising will usually be read only by those who are seeking another job, whereas radio advertising at peak commuting time may catch the attention of a listener driving to or from work and may spark their interest to find out more. Care needs to be taken, however, with the response since it is much easier to respond to written advertisements, where all the information on response address etc is ready to hand, whereas television, cinema and radio advertising passes very rapidly and people may not have the opportunity to take down the full details.

Interactive advertising

The internet has revolutionised the world of computing and has now spread to advertising. The internet offers many of the advantages of cinema, television and radio advertising without the disadvantages of cost and speed. Internet advertisements can be prepared in-house and placed on the web almost immediately. The web is in essence a section of the computer network which will hold the 'pages' of the advertisement for users of the internet to read. Anyone with access to the internet can have access to the information. This can be particularly effective for international recruitment campaigns. In the same way that live advertising can catch the attention of people not seeking job advertisements, so too can the internet catch those who are 'browsing' other information on the service. It also has the added advantage of the potential to link up with other pieces of information about the company. The restrictions of space and cost associated with newspaper and live advertising are not prohibitive with on-line advertising. There is generally little limitation on space and it is possible therefore to put together a few pages of information and, where the organisation has other web sites on its products, services etc, these can be linked to provide much greater detail. This is comparable to sending out product brochures and the company annual report with every application form. The cost is restricted to the development of the information on the web site. The cost of accessing the information is borne by the 'reader'.

Since the internet is a multimedia facility, it provides the opportunity to have the best of both worlds in giving written information one would find in static advertising with photographs and/or video images to supplement the information, and thereby achieve the impact of live advertising. A further advantage of this approach is that application forms can be sent through the system either by placing the form on the web or forwarding it by electronic mail (e-mail). When the e-mail system is used a candidate can access the form, provide information on themselves and return it direct. In the same way that the advertiser can include static and live information so too can the candidate return photographs or video images, which may be particularly useful when looking at evidence of creative ability. The potential savings in printing and postage on a large-scale campaign can also be beneficial. The internet can be a very effective means of advertising for certain kinds of staff, particularly those who are likely to be users of the internet. In the early days of the internet this was undoubtedly confined to the 'anorak brigade' but the rapid rise in affordability and accessibility of on-line computing is rapidly expanding the potential labour marketplace. The disadvantage is that the internet may not be suitable for all kinds of positions and is very much a wide-spread medium, indeed truly global.

A more traditional form of interactive advertising is the use of a recruitment event, whether in conjunction with others (such as a recruitment fair), or dedicated (such as an open evening by the company). In this form of advertising, candidates are encouraged to come along and browse the information with the company and this can take the form of written material, together with static displays and stands and perhaps a video presentation of the company, its products, and employment opportunities, and perhaps supplemented by live presentations or demonstrations. A particular benefit of this approach is that it enables a wide range of information to be fed to potential candidates in helping them to make their choice. It also filters out weak applications, in that those who make the effort to attend are more likely to be truly interested. The downside is that it can be expensive to stage events, particularly if third party facilities are being used, such as a hotel, and it requires significant resources from the company in terms of staff availability etc. It offers the added advantage, however, of being able to be integrated seamlessly with other parts of the selection process so that it may encompass the completion of application forms during the event and may also include informal interviewing or discussion.

Advertising agencies

It is possible 'to go it alone' with the employment marketing strategy, or with any other element related to the process of attracting candidates. It is particularly tempting, where a low level of local recruitment is being undertaken, to draft and place advertisements directly. The use of an advertising agency may seem an extravagance but it is an area in which any time and money will be well invested. In the simple placing of advertisements, many agencies will work free of charge, using discounts negotiated from the media to 'subsidise' the work undertaken for the client. Sometimes agencies will pass on part of the discount to the client. The benefits of using an agency extend beyond simply the creativity and technical expertise that they can provide. Although this in itself is valuable in reinforcing a proper image of the organisation, some of the greatest benefits come from the process of explaining requirements to the agency. The need to crystallise and present thoughts on the candidate requirements, the opportunities the role affords, the current state of the organisation, etc, provide an invaluable step in preparing to lay such information before applicants in a clear and attractive fashion. Furthermore, it is extremely rare to find an agency being profligate with the client's advertising budget; it is almost universally true that agencies will take great time and care in advising the client on the best possible use of cost-effective media. The use of a well-drafted and attractive advertisement (or any other form of announcement) will pay dividends in improving the response ratio – ie raising the proportion of candidates who are more suited to the role and reducing the proportion and number of unsuitable applications. It is also, of course, far more efficient for selectors to be devoting their time to selection activities rather than trying to master copywriting or layout skills.

In choosing an advertising agency, it would be appropriate to seek evidence of previous assignments undertaken, and the way in which they were handled. In showing examples of any previous work, the agency should be able to demonstrate how it took the brief and developed a strategy aimed at the target audience, how the advertising was received by that audience, and be able to provide specific measures of response rate, selection ratios and other statistics to illustrate the success of their work. A clever or visually appealing advertisement may be evidence of a very creative mind but creativity, although important, is less important than suitability.

9

SCREENING

Screening

A well-developed method of attracting candidates to apply to
the organisation, whether it be a carefully drafted and comprehensive advertisement or any of the other methods mentioned in the earlier chapter on attracting candidates, will be
effective in improving the response quality. That is to say,
the proportion of potentially suitable candidates will be
increased, and unsuitable candidates will be deterred or will
select themselves out, thereby reducing the overall number of
candidates. The thrust of the attraction process should therefore be to bring in a smaller total number of applications with
a higher proportion of suitable applicants.

However good the attraction process, it is highly likely that
there will be more candidates than positions to be filled and
often (but not always) the case that there will be more candidates than can be realistically taken on to the next stage of
more time-consuming selection processes such as interviewing or testing etc. A screening process will therefore be needed
to distil the full response of applicants to a manageable
number of candidates for further, more detailed, consideration.

There is not always a need for a screening process. In some
instances there may be a very small number of candidates for
positions and the use of a screening technique may be unnecessary. This may seem an obvious point, but it frequently
occurs that speculative applicants for a hard-to-fill vacancy are
asked to complete an application form, which may delay or
even deter progress of the application when, in practice, the

application form will be a less useful method of selection than an interview, test, or other assessment process which could be set up immediately. Screening techniques should therefore usually be considered not as a means of improving the selection decision but rather as a means of refining the volume of applications into a manageable quantity.

There are two main views of screening; there are those who approach it as a means of screening out and those who approach it as a means of screening-in. The screening-out school of thought looks for any aspects within the application form etc that will provide an 'excuse' to reject the candidate. The screening-in school of thought will review the application and attempt to draw conclusions, albeit preliminary, on the candidate's suitability for the post. This may seem a subtle distinction, but in practice it is a very important and fundamental difference in approach, which will impact greatly on the efficacy of the selection process. In general the screening-out approach will prove far less effective and more damaging than screening-in. The screening-in approach will be to use key criteria, usually competencies, derived from the role analysis and related to the person-specification. The application form etc will be assessed to identify whether there is any evidence that the applicant matches the criteria. There are various degrees of sophistication to this process, which are described under the techniques below. The screening-out approach is less person-oriented and more process-oriented. It is concerned with reducing the number of forms rather than the number of people. Anecdotally, the screening out-approach is likely to entail the selector discarding an application because it is completed in blue ink when the instructions required black, or typed when the instructions specified hand-written. These may, of course, be perfectly valid objections if the organisation is looking for people who are not innovators, not risk takers and have neat handwriting, and where the organisation does not want to embark on the not-so-complex task of training people to use black ink ('this is a black pen, use it') or has a legally defensible requirement to discriminate against colour-blind people. Assuming these things are valid, however, it may be that they have been allowed to override more important criteria, and potentially suitable candidates may be rejected before there is an opportunity to consider fully and evaluate some of their other criteria. It is, of course, easy to criticise such approaches but it should not be overlooked that they often occur when there is a very high number of applications, perhaps several thousand, a pressing time deadline and very limited resources to handle the task. In such circumstances care needs to be given to improving the attraction techniques, automating the selection process, or increasing the availability of resources. The importance of the screening process cannot be over-emphasised because later selection techniques can only help to identify the potential of the candidates in the available pool – they will not improve the quality of the pool itself.

The main techniques for screening are:

- application forms and CVs
- telephone screening
- biodata.

In recent years some organisations have also resorted to random techniques for screening such as the use of computer-generated random selection of candidate numbers or pulling names out of a hat. Incredible though it may seem, such techniques have found favour with a number of responsible organisations, including some public sector organisations, as a means of handling high volumes of applications. They are, however, lotteries rather than selection techniques and are not deserving of attention in any serious consideration of recruitment and selection.

Application forms and curricula vitae

One of the most popular tools in recruitment and selection is the written (or printed) application. Studies have shown that it is used in 98 per cent of selection projects. It has become so much a part of recruitment custom that it is wholly expected by candidates and taken for granted by most recruiters. The written application can either take the form of a standard application form or a curriculum vitae (CV).

The CV approach allows the candidate to develop his or her own format and send the information they consider appropriate in the way in which they feel is appropriate. It is generally used for more senior positions where the use of a standard form is frowned upon as a somewhat clerical activity for senior people to be engaged in. One of the advantages of the CV approach is that it is speedier and less costly because there is no delay in sending out an application form, and the cost of its postage is avoided. Some recruiters prefer to use the CV because it demonstrates the ability of the candidate to marshal their thoughts and put together a clear piece of communication. The disadvantage of a CV is that it enables the candidate to construct the application to inflate their strong points and obscure or omit any weakness or concerns. It is also the case that some 'professional applicants' can print off many copies and send them indiscriminately to organisations, whereas the work involved in completing the application form would test their resolve and therefore their seriousness.

The standard application form is the most common technique for screening applications. Ideally each application form should be designed around the role to be recruited. In practice this is unlikely to be feasible and, depending on the size of the organisation and diversity of roles, there may be a single uniform application form or a small number of forms for different job families. The application form is probably one of the most maligned and misused recruitment tools. With careful design and proper attention it can become an extremely effective part of the overall selection process. The application form should be considered as an investigative tool rather than a piece of protocol. It should be designed to elicit information in the same way that an interview or any other recruitment tool provides a vehicle for candidates to supply answers in response to questions. It should therefore be designed very much with the purpose of the questions in mind. Thought also needs to be given both to the ergonomics of the form, in the sense of ease of completion by candidates, and to its visual impact since it may be one of the first impressions of the company that the candidate receives. It is generally better to marshal the questions into homogeneous blocks. So, for example, personal information such as name, address, contact number etc will be in one section, information on work record and experience will be in another, educational qualifications or professional qualifications will be in yet another, and so on. Within each section it is more sensible for the information to be provided in chronological order since it becomes much easier to assess the application.

The written application needs, of course, to fulfil a number of purposes. On the one hand it will be the reference document used for the contact address, phone number etc of the candidate and will become an integral part of the administration of the selection process. It will also form a guide for vetting the candidates prior to appointment; so that claimed qualifications can be checked, work records confirmed, medical conditions verified, and references taken up, etc. The form will also be used in preparation for the interview and as a means of framing interview questions around key points of information in the form. Finally, the key purpose of the form will be to provide information on which decisions can be made on whether or not to take people forward to the next stage of the selection process. It is worth bearing in mind these different uses of the form when designing it, since different people will be accessing different parts of the form, and efficiencies of processing can be particularly important in dealing with large volumes of recruitment applications.

In order to ease administrative burdens on the management of recruitment and selection many organisations have now automated the administrative process. There are many computer software packages which combine a word-processing and database mail-merge facility so that the name and contact address of the candidate can be entered on to the system once only and then called up from the database to produce acknowledgement letters, invitations to interview, rejection letters etc at the appropriate stage without the need to re-enter the data, giving a personalised letter to all candidates even though the computer will generate hundreds or thousands of identical letters. In order to use automated processes it is necessary to allocate a number or other identifier to candidates and some organisations have taken this a stage further in using bar-codes to identify candidates, and 'assemble' information from a range of sources including the test results, application form, interview results etc by using the bar-code system.

A more recent form of automation is the use of the internet. In its early days it may have been the domain of 'computer nerds' but its general use and acceptability has become common-place in the USA and is becoming more so in the UK. It is, of course, less novel to younger people and is therefore very suitable for graduate recruitment. A review of traditional application response times by Hewlett-Packard in the USA showed that 'good' job-seekers could obtain a new post within a week, but the cycle time for recruitment was over 50 days; which meant that 'good' candidates were not caught in time. The internet allows a radical reduction in candidate response time, immediate screener access and faster employer response time. The improved cycle time enables the quality of response to be improved. The internet can also work by allowing the candidate to submit an electronic CV or complete an electronic application form.

It may seem an obvious point – but one that is missed, judging by the design of some application forms – that the form should be 'road-tested' to ensure that there is sufficient space for people to complete the information requested of them and that the instructions are clear. Forms are never easy to complete by those who are not involved in the design, and the use of correct simple terminology, boxes, lines and shading all help the candidate. Colour is an important consideration, particularly where a large volume of forms will need to be read. Black ink on a yellow background is the most legible of all colour combinations and professional form designers will be able to advise on these and other aspects. Many application forms still use headings rather than questions to seek information. For some roles such as blue collar work where form filling may be more unusual and perhaps intimidating, some organisations have found it successful to use the approach of a questionnaire rather than a form so that the headings are phrased as questions for candidates to answer.

Although the screening of applications is an important part of the process, for many organisations it is an unstructured part. It is also a part of the process that selectors often feel can be delegated to junior staff. It is the case, however, that the unstructured approach is also the hit-and-miss approach. For some reason it is common in organisations to overlook the time needed to review application forms and there are many occasions where recruiters find themselves sifting through large volumes of applications on their lap in front of the evening television. For some it is difficult to delegate this aspect of the work if junior staff do not have sufficient experience to make selection decisions. There are, however, techniques that can help considerably to improve the screening process. It is, of course, a necessary prerequisite to have a very clear person-specification and this is more helpful if it is expressed in the form of competencies. Taking the framework outlined in Chapter 5, the application should focus on the acquired and adapting competencies. The *acquired* would be the knowledge and experience. Knowledge can be specified in terms of qualifications and these can be checked through the application form; experience can similarly be specified by reference to a number of years, perhaps a type of industry or organisation or company, and the nature of the role. The *adapting* competencies will look at the way in which the individual has applied their talent to different circumstances or situations, and the more senior the appointment the more the screener will look for evidence of achievement in different settings. Very often some of these competencies are very easy to specify; there may be, for example, the requirement for a driving licence, a typing qualification, an accountancy qualification or experience of shift working, or of dealing with members of the public, etc. As part of the screening process the competencies that are to be assessed at this stage should be identified and prioritised as appropriate. This is likely to be a small number of competencies – perhaps not more than six. These should then be given a weighting so that the total score of the competencies comes to a hundred. A simple rating system, perhaps four-scale, should be used which will, for example, identify whether the application:

- shows no evidence of the competency
- shows some evidence of the competency
- shows full evidence of the competency
- shows evidence of the competency displayed at higher levels than this role.

Examples are then provided to the screener of what is meant by the competency at each of these levels.

Taking a hypothetical example, one of the competencies may be *technical knowledge* which may have been defined as 'human resource management' and described as 'provides guidance to line management in the application of existing procedures for the management of staff, including selection, discipline, grievance and performance management procedures . . .' which would be further qualified in the person specification as 'evidenced by three to four years as HR or personnel officer . . .'. This would then be anchored as the third level in the example rating so that:

- the application form showing that the individual operated as HR officer giving general advice would go into rating 2 because there is some evidence but it does not indicate that they were involved in all the aspects such as selection, discipline etc
- someone giving the specified examples would go into rating 3
- someone showing they were responsible for designing, developing, implementing and advising on some of those policies would go into rating 4
- someone with no experience in HR would be on rating 1.

Thus, the competencies are derived from the competency framework and the screener simply applies a rating scale which can have as many ratings as desired. Given that competencies in organisations are usually described in a way that lend themselves to observation and such observation will, of course, be unavailable at the time of screening, it is important to add those additional descriptors such as 'three to four years experience of . . .'. Continuing with this example, if the technical knowledge had been weighted at 40 points and the candidate had been rated at three, they would have scored 120 points. The process is repeated for the remainder of the competencies to be screened and a total score obtained (see Table 7). The degree to which this screening process is simple or complex is governed by the number of competencies chosen and the number of ratings used. It does ensure, however, that there is a consistency to the screening process.

Table 7

RATING AN APPLICATION THROUGH THE WEIGHTED COMPETENCIES METHOD

Competency	Weight	Rating	Score
Technical knowledge	40	3	120
Business knowledge	30	4	120
Results	20	4	80
People experience	10	2	20
TOTAL			340

In many organisations where an unstructured approach is used there is very little consistency in the screening process and it is often the case that the selection is based upon the perceptions and values of the screener, who may not be representative of the values and aspirations of the kind of person being sought. A simple test that organisations can use to check the consistency of screening is to provide the same set of applications to a range of different people who are asked to create a shortlist (without conferring). In the unstructured process it is highly likely that the shortlists will be different. The use of a structured scoring system may appear at first to be more complex, but it simplifies and speeds the process significantly in addition to improving consistency and defensibility. Additionally, the use of such scoring enables the cut-off point to be adjusted to allow for greater or fewer numbers to proceed to the next stage according to the specific circumstances of each selection assignment.

The structured screening process can be used with any application form but it is particularly suitable where the form has been designed with this process in mind. Some organisations therefore construct the application form so that there are sections on the screened competency. In these sections the applicant is given the definition of the competency and perhaps some examples to help them understand and they then have a free text box in which to convey information that will enable the screener to identify their level of competency in that regard. Table 8 shows how this works for three of the eight competencies required by applicants to the Passport Agency. This system is not only fairer to candidates but is much easier for selectors since it prompts the candidate to provide the information that is essential for undertaking effective screening of their application. It is in some ways a significant move towards self-screening.

Job questionnaires

An additional technique, although not screening in the strict sense, that can assist in the objective of reducing the numbers at this stage, is the use of job questionnaires (JQs). It has been shown that information given to applicants is not always read. In one case study of graduate recruits it was found that the company brochure (rather glossy and expensive) was not read by applicants until the night before their interview as a means of 'revision'. It did not influence their decision to submit or withhold their application for employment. It was therefore an unnecessary cost for the organisation, not simply in terms of the cost of the brochure itself but also of the additional cost of postage and administration. Conversely, job questionnaires have been shown to be influential on people in forming their decision to submit or withhold their application. The job questionnaire takes the form of a number of questions which are a self-scored quiz similar in form to the light-hearted questionnaires found in popular leisure magazines. The applicant answers the question, scores in accordance with the instructions, and then proceeds to read the answer and check against the scoring key. Thus the questionnaire may be along the lines of:

Q1   The job of the sales clerk means frequent contact with potential and existing customers.
True or false?

Table 8
EXTRACT FROM THE PASSPORT AGENCY'S APPLICATION FORM

About your qualities, skills and attributes

Communication

Communication in the Passport Agency is about • conveying information clearly, accurately and convincingly both orally and in writing and • recognising the importance of listening and understanding the needs of others.

Please give an example of a time when you have shown one or more of the qualities, skills and attributes outlined in the 'Communications' section of the person specification enclosed with this form.

Customer care

Customer care in the Passport Agency is about • showing a desire to address the needs of others and make customer care a priority and • paying close attention to internal and external customer needs with the aim of establishing effective relationships and 'partnerships'.

Please give an example of a time when you have shown one or more of the qualities, skills and attributes outlined in the 'Customer care' section of the person specification enclosed with this form.

Productivity and quality

Productivity and quality in the Passport Agency is about • showing urgency to get things done and completing tasks effectively to the required timescales and targets and • getting things right first time, being thorough, methodical and consistently spotting mistakes.

Please give an example of a time when you have shown one or more of the qualities, skills and attributes outlined in the 'Productivity and quality' section of the person specification enclosed with this form.

Reproduced with the permission of the UK Passport Agency

The applicant is faced with a range of these questions, perhaps 15 or 20, to which they will answer 'true' or 'false'. They
will then go to the scoring key which will tell them that the
answer to Q1 is false, and to score 1 if they answered 'false',
score 0 if they answered 'true'. There then follows a short
statement which gives information about that answer. For
example, 'False. The key contact from the company for customers is the sales representative through whom all relationships should be conducted. The sales clerk will mainly be
working with the sales representatives and routing all queries
through them, although there may be occasions when a customer query has to be handled directly. The thrust of this role
is not on relationships but on making sure that the sales doc-
umentation is properly processed, that the information on the
customer's account is properly maintained, and linked
through to the invoicing procedures . . .' etc. Similar information is provided for each of the questions and because the
applicants have tested, they are interested in seeing the result.
They then total all the scores and look at a ready reckoner
which will say something along the lines of:

Score 8 or less.
This role may not be right for you, it may not offer the challenges or opportunities you were looking for and you should
think very carefully before proceeding any further with the
application.

Score 8 to 13.
This role may be different from the way in which you originally envisaged it. Think carefully before you proceed and
read further information in the attached job description or
contact the recruitment selection help line on....., before proceeding with your application.

Score 14 to 20.
This role could be just what you are looking for. Take a look
through the enclosed job description and information, and
complete and return the form within the next week so that
we have the opportunity to give your application full consideration.

In this way applicants are helped to screen themselves out of the process without the adverse consequences of rejection and without the organisation incurring the cost of dealing with the returned application. In times of high unemployment there will always be 'desperation applications', but JQs are still a very valuable tool for reducing unsuitable applications.

Telephone screening

One of the recent advances in screening has been the use of telephone screening. This is particularly suitable for those roles which will involve telephone contact, such as help line positions etc. It works through advertising the positions and inviting applicants to telephone a certain number, perhaps during a certain time, but all within a defined period of perhaps days or weeks. Applicants ring to find out more about the job but they are answered by an operator who has a script incorporating a set of questions and a scoring system similar to that described in the scored application form above. This system may be a manual system but is more often a computer-based scoring which also operates a response log. The response log is particularly appropriate where a number of operators are assigned to handle a large volume of telephone calls. This means the scoring is performed on-screen by the operator during the telephone call, the system will undertake the calculation but, more importantly, will provide the operator with information on whether that candidate's score puts them among the top respondents, the middle, or the bottom etc and therefore helps to direct the next stage. The next stage is for the operator to place the applicant on the fast or slow track. The 'fast track' is for the applicant to be asked to proceed to the next stage, which may be either a face-to-face interview or being asked to telephone again at a set time and date to engage in a more lengthy discussion which will form a telephone interview. The computer-based logging system will help the operator to give the appropriate slot to the applicant. Information may be sent simultaneously to the applicant, including a standard application form or other company details, although the process may render some or all of that activity unnecessary.

The 'slow track' is where the applicant is advised that a pack will be sent to them in the post which will contain further information and an application form. It can be, but rarely is, the case that the applicant is advised that their application will not be suitable. It is rare because of the adverse reaction to being rejected 'over the phone'. Sending out information to the applicants therefore enables them to believe that their application will still be considered and overcomes the potential adverse reactions, while not disrupting the selection process which is continuing for the 'fast track' applicants. Furthermore, there is the opportunity of a 'safety net' to consider submitted applications further, if required, using the structured screening approach.

The telephone screening approach has many advantages. It is particularly useful where the positions being considered involve a high level of telephone activity and where it is extremely difficult to assess such skills from an application form but where such skills may be so fundamental as to rule out the candidate. It is a very speedy process and controls the rate at which applicants respond in a way that written applications cannot, given the timing of the postal system. It also has the advantage of building a personal bond with the organisation; a telephone call of even the most clinical nature tends to be seen as far more personal than the most carefully drafted and warm letter. The disadvantages are primarily logistics and cost. It may not be possible to predict fully and accurately the scale of response and put sufficient operators on duty to answer the calls. It will, of course, need dedicated telephone lines and a number of operators to answer and this usually means manning such lines outside normal office hours. There is also the requirement to create an effective script and scoring mechanism and this can be quite costly when an automated scoring mechanism and logging and diary system is used. It is likely to be beyond the scope and resources of most HR departments to mount such an operation internally but it is quite feasible to use third party resources successfully for such an exercise. While there may be some cost savings in the avoidance of postage and printing costs for sending out applications and other information, these cannot be avoided entirely and such savings are still likely to be less than the cost of mounting the operation. Cost considerations will therefore remain the key constraint on widespread use of this approach. There are few other problems with this approach; most people nowadays have access to telephones, and providing the opportunity to call at out-of-hours times avoids further difficulties. There are some hidden advantages in that it avoids some of the problems of discrimination, particularly of race and disability, since the telephone call may give no indication of these.

As yet there has been no indication that organisations will be taking this a stage further into 'cold calling', by targeting people, using information available to many organisations engaged in cold-calling activities, and persuading them to apply. Sandwiched between the early-evening phone calls, from the bank calling to offer its latest insurance scheme and the ubiquitous double glazing salesmen, there may yet be organisations phoning about their employment offerings, but to date this kind of activity has been limited to executive search consultants.

Biodata

Biodata is a technique that is rarely used in selection, yet it does well on all measures of effectiveness. Biodata is an abbreviation of 'biographical data' and is the process by which the story of people's lives will hold keys to their future. It uses the simple assumption that past actions, behaviours, etc will be the best predictor of future behaviours, patterns, etc. Biodata as a concept is not new, nor is it particularly unfamiliar outside of the selection process. Most people are accustomed to being asked to complete questions about themselves when they apply for bank loans, credit cards or car insurance, etc. Most people are aware that the premium they pay for their car insurance will be linked to their history of incident-free driving and their age, and the make and model of car. It is well known that a 20-year-old male driver of a two-seater sports car with a recent history of accidents and claims will pay a higher premium than a 50-year-old driver with a clean record and driving a family saloon. Similarly, most people are aware that the postcode of their home will have a significant bearing on the amount of home contents premium they pay and will be used by insurance companies to gauge the probability of burglary at their homes. In the information age, our address, age and occupation can help political parties predict our affiliations, help supermarkets plan location of their new stores, help marketers decide which products to inform us about, and help financial institutions to decide the degree of risk we may pose. It is not surprising, therefore, that the history of biodata began with insurance companies that are accustomed to using biographical information for decision-making.

The earliest recorded use of biodata was with Chicago underwriters in 1894, when Colonel Thomas Peters of the Washington Life Insurance Company used biodata to improve the selection of life assurance agents. In the same way that Peters used biodata for insurance calculations so he took data on successful and unsuccessful insurance salesmen to attempt to predict the likelihood of them succeeding and staying in their particular role. The process was taken a stage further in the 1920s when another insurance company looked at 500 people selling life assurance and focused on 50 good, 50 poor, and 50 'middling' salesmen from the sample and analysed their application forms. The researcher looked at all the basic information on the form, such as age, marital status, education, experience etc, together with the response to the question 'what amount of insurance are you confident of placing each month?'. The researcher looked at whether the candidate replied to the question, not at the reply itself. By careful correlation it was possible to see what items distinguished good from 'middling', and 'middling' from bad. Each of these factors was then assigned a set of scores to be used in weighting the rating of their response. This was turned into a 'weighted application blank' (WAB). This is in some ways similar to the structured screening format for application forms but differs in that the form itself is structured solely around these aspects, is not based on any analysis of roles but on the 'coincidences' of successful people, and adopts a fairly complex scoring process.

In modern biodata methods there are two main approaches:

- weighted application blanks (WAB)
- rational biodata.

Weighted application blanks are used more extensively in recruitment in the USA than they are in the UK. They are particularly prevalent for military service, being used by both the US Navy and the US Army, and by department stores and manufacturers. The WAB has been called 'mindlessly empirical' by its critics since it takes the significant differences, applies a weighting and uses the result regardless of any understanding of why it should exist. It may say that 23 year old employees with dark hair living in post codes X and Y who play tennis and enjoy going to the cinema and live at home with their parents and own a certain make of car are more effective at serving on the sales counter, or whatever, than those who do not fit that description. It is, in essence, coincidence that determines and predicts suitability rather than any understandable criteria. Because it is derived from the existing differences in performance it cannot be constructed from the ground up but can only be constructed by looking at the differences that exist.

It can be argued that this approach is absolutely fair in the sense that it concerns itself only with those factors which differentiate between different levels of performance and uses them to drive selection decisions. In practice, people tend to feel uncomfortable with the unexplained factors and somehow feel that it is 'unfair'. This has, perhaps, been one of the most important barriers to the further growth of weighted application blanks for general use. Curiously in some ways, it is not an altogether new process in that many seasoned recruiters will have preferences, when looking through application forms, for certain schools or universities citing that previous people recruited from those institutions were perhaps better performers or stayed longer than those from other institutions. The same is often said about certain neighbourhoods. Interestingly, the danger of prejudice and subjectivity creeping in to such judgements should make them more uncomfortable than the mechanistic approach of the WABs, yet it doesn't seem to be so in practice.

To take a biodata example: during World War II the United States Airforce used comprehensive selection techniques to predict success in flight training for pilots. The techniques included a complete battery of psychological tests, interviews, and assessment exercises, together with a biodata which included, among others, the question 'Did you ever build a model aeroplane that flew?' At first sight it seems rather strange to be asking grown men (and it was exclusively men at that time) questions about their boyhood activities, particularly given the seriousness of the task for which they were being selected. Yet it was the case that that single question was almost as good a predictor of success for flight training as the entire test battery.

The rational biodata is to the untrained eye little different to the empirical biodata of the weighted application blank. It differs, however, in its approach and is therefore a fundamental shift. In principle, it attempts to avoid using coincidences mindlessly but instead tries to identify the factors, seek some explanation of them, and then construct questions designed to identify those factors. Thus in this approach, using a competency framework in which one of the competencies is perhaps decision-making, the biodata would set out to ask questions which correlated with the levels of decision-making in high-performing, average, and low-performing employees. Using this approach, the biographical information which diagnosed the level of decision-making in applicants would form the question to be incorporated in the biodata. In practice this would mean incorporating a number of questions around decision-making in the same way that a psychological test would be constructed to avoid over-reliance on one question alone. As a consequence, the biodata would reveal whether the patterns of the applicant's life matched the patterns in the lives of those people in the organisation who were good at decision-making. It would not, however, identify whether they would be able to make different types of decision from those people or whether they would perform significantly better, slightly better or slightly worse, whether they would be consistent in their decision-making, or the style in which they would go about their decision-making. It would simply indicate that they are likely to be decision-makers in the same mould as those whom the organisation currently regards as good at decision-making. It therefore goes some way towards providing a rationale for the process but it still remains a largely inexplicable technique.

Designing biodata

The design of biodata using weighted application blanks is as follows. The first stage is to develop a set of questions to be put to applicants with the application form. These are open-ended questions which may, for example, have one question asking 'what are your interests or hobbies?' This is given on a trial basis to applicants along with the existing application form or whatever other method is used. When a sufficiently large response has been received the forms can be analysed to identify the most frequent responses; thus under the question on interests it may be that football, hockey, netball, cinema, gardening, reading, television and stamp collecting are the most frequent responses. The next stage is to turn the open questions into closed questions and create a modified form which would now ask the question 'please indicate which hobbies you have: gardening, swimming etc'. It is, of course, essential in order to get to the closed questions, that the open question form should have encompassed a whole raft of issues of every conceivable biographical kind. The closed questionnaire is then used alongside existing selection methods but the responses are stored and tracked over a period of time to identify which people stayed with the organisation and which people were more likely to be shortlisted, which were more likely to succeed, etc. This needs to be undertaken over a period of time, usually about three to five years. An extract from a typical biodata form (developed for a client by CGR) appears in Table 9.

At the end of the study period it may, for example, be shown that the hobbies or interests of people bore no correlation with whether they were shortlisted, did well at the interview, stayed longer or performed better. In that case this factor would be removed from the final biodata form. It may be the case, however, that swimming, watching television and netball correlated highly with those who stayed or with those who performed well, or both. In that case the interest question would remain on the form and those three responses would receive a plus score to identify a correlation. It may be that one of the responses, perhaps football, correlated strongly with those people who did not stay long in the job or who did not perform well, and it would then receive a negative score. The remaining interests can either be removed from the form and subsumed under 'other' or remain on the form and receive a neutral, ie zero, score. The final form will therefore be not only a form but a scoring mechanism and scores will be allocated to the different responses that people make. The final scores will then determine whether people will be brought forward in the selection process.

Some organisations are not prepared to wait a number of years to develop biodata, and therefore issue the form to existing staff, correlate it with their performance ratings and make assumptions on that basis. There are some dangers in this approach because the response to these questions will change after people have joined the organisation, but it can nevertheless be a useful short cut to developing the biodata form.

The development of the rational biodata differs slightly in that the initial form would not be a scatter-gun approach to identifying every conceivable biographical element. Instead it would begin by taking the competencies identified in the organisation and framing a set of questions linked to identifying responses indicative of those competencies. The correlation and scoring aspects would, however, be the same for both WAB and the rational biodata. It is implicit in this process, of course, that correlations need to be statistically significant in order to be useful and that the population size on which the research is based should also be sufficiently large to produce meaningful results.

The development of biodata can be a slow process, and it can also be an expensive process. Once completed, however, it offers a number of advantages in improving the selection process. As can be seen in Chapter 7, on choosing techniques, it is an effective predictor of success, higher in some studies than personality tests or interviewing or the traditional methods of screening applications; it could therefore obviate existing processes. It could, for example, be used alone, eliminating application forms, testing, interviewing etc. Alternatively, it could be used simply as a screening process, as an effective means of reducing applications to a manageable number. There is, however, a difficulty with the biodata in this approach in that it may be a more effective predictor of performance than is the interview. Yet the interviewer may see from the interview that person A is far

Table 9
EXTRACT FROM A TYPICAL BIODATA FORM

Further education

I **Which of these factors influenced the choice of university to which you applied?** (Mark all which apply)

[ ] Academic reputation of university
[ ] Academic reputation of the course
[ ] Type of course (e.g. vocational, sandwich)
[ ] Location
[ ] Reputation for social life
[ ] Sporting opportunities
[ ] Opportunities for study overseas offered by course
[ ] Other (please specify)

2 **Which type of teaching did you find most effective for you while studying for your degree?** (Mark one box only)

[ ] A Loosely supervised researched (individual or group)
[ ] B Lectures and essays on set topics
[ ] C Seminars/discussions
[ ] D Personal tuition
[ ] E Other (please specify)

3 **Typically, how did you prepare for your degree examinations?** (Mark one box only)

[ ] A With a scheduled revision programme on all topics
[ ] B Revision of weak areas over the last month or so
[ ] C Prepared a few expected topics in depth
[ ] D Crash revision in the last couple of weeks
[ ] E None of these

Leisure activities

4 **Mark all of the following that you are ACTIVELY involved in (i.e. at least weekly)**

[ ] Playing a team sport
[ ] Individual sport (e.g. athletics)
[ ] Going to parties, pubs, clubs etc.
[ ] Socialising with friends in a group
[ ] Practical hobbies (e.g. repairing bikes, cars etc)
[ ] Creative or artistic hobbies
[ ] Outdoor pursuits (e.g. climbing, sailing etc)
[ ] Amateur dramatics/acting/singing
[ ] Voluntary, charitable, religious activities
[ ] Computing as a serious hobby e.g. Internet, programming
[ ] Playing computer games
[ ] Reading
[ ] Watching TV/cinema
[ ] Other (please specify)

5 **How often do you go out with a group of friends, socially or to places of interest?**

[ ] Most evenings
[ ] Once or twice a week
[ ] Once or twice a month
[ ] Seldom

more suitable than person B. The biodata measures person B to be far more suitable than person A. Since the interview is entirely rational (it is hoped) and the biodata is entirely empirical it is impossible to explain or reconcile the differences. The biodata will be proven to be more effective than the interview as a means of predicting performance. In practice, however, the interviewer will dismiss person B in favour of person A and in so doing also dismiss the biodata as a short-listing mechanism because it is out of tune with their rational judgements. In this case, of course, the biodata is not only more effective but also more objective than the interview.

One of the limitations of biodata is its shelf-life. It will be only a matter of time before word gets around that 'to get a job in that organisation you need to be good at tennis' etc; it can therefore be capable of manipulation and will need to be revisited every few years and amended, which of course carries a cost implication. Biodata provides the opportunity to fully automate the process using the biodata as an alternative to the application form which can be read through an optical character recognition machine that can score in a second or less. This, in turn, can be linked to a computer selection software package to trigger rejection letters, invitations to interview, etc. At first it may seem a discomforting scenario but compared to random selection or subjective vagaries it is both fair to the candidates and effective for the organisation.

One of the greatest difficulties facing biodata is the perception of applicants. Although we may be accustomed to insurance premiums and junk mail being determined from biographical data we are less happy about job prospects being so determined. Where it is employed it should therefore be printed as an adjunct to a traditional-looking application form and its use carefully explained as being a means of matching the preferences and expectations of the applicant with the organisation and the teams within which he or she will be working.

The conditions for successful use of biodata set out by Gunter, Furnham and Drakely are:

- The criteria for job success or acceptability must be defined clearly.

Some people will use biodata to predict whether people are likely to stay with the organisation, others use it to predict whether they are likely to be successful in performance. Some use it for both. When it comes to performance there must be a very clear idea of what is meant by performance. On paper it seems a simple matter, in practice it is anything but simple. Gaining agreement among sales managers of who is the most successful sales-person, among bank managers of who is a successful lender, and among universities of who is the most successful academic, is far from straightforward. Performance ratings are notoriously bad as indicators of performance. The criteria need to be accurately established if reliance is to be placed on the biodata identifying them.

- The target jobs should be relatively homogeneous.

In large or complex organisations where a range of job roles is to be found covering, for example, sales, manufacturing, clerical and professional and advisory roles it is unlikely that a common set of criteria can be established to cover all those roles. In such circumstances it may be possible to use the same biodata form but the defining criteria and the scoring mechanism underlying the form will be different for each of the groups.

- The likely candidates for the job should be of broadly similar age and background.

This is not so much set as a prerequisite for successful development of biodata as an observation on the experiences of those who have developed biodata thus far. It flows from the concern that if asking questions framed around university degrees, for example, such questions will have a different connotation for younger people where access to higher education has been more available than it will for an older population where such access was constrained by social background. Similarly, care needs to be taken in developing the biodata to avoid building in any cultural discriminators, particularly where they may be racially discriminatory. Framing questions around party-going would for example be difficult for Muslim women to answer in the same way as others.

- Researchers should have access to large development and cross-validation samples.

The recommendation from Gunter, Furnham and Drakeley (1993) is that a sample size should be about 500 people for development purposes and, assuming that 50 to 70 per cent of the original questions (or items within questions) correlate with performance, a further 250 to 350 for cross-validation. This underlines the potential complexity and cost of biodata development.

- If part of an application blank (form), a biodata must be in a format acceptable to candidates.

This point was made earlier but Gunter, Furnham and Drakeley point out that not all candidates are hostile to the biodata appearance and that in one organisation, engineering graduates found a multiple choice biodata a refreshing change from the 'burden of writing florid prose in response to the usual open ended questions'.

- People must be aware of what constitutes success in using biodata.

This is key to the acceptability of biodata as a selection tool by recruiters. It is not easy for recruiters to accept the 'black box' principle of biodata and they feel uncomfortable in accepting decisions which are not accompanied by any rational explanation or theory. It is understanding that biodata will not predict interview performance or test performance – it will predict job performance and it therefore sits as a competitor to other techniques rather than a complementor.

Given the nature of biodata it is probably most likely to be used as an alternative to applications in large volume frequent recruitment rather than as an alternative to aspects such as interviewing, testing, etc and although it can be seen as a selection tool, its attractiveness is more likely to be as a screening tool. It is also worth remembering that biodata can be used as a predictor of various measures, which include performance but also absenteeism, job tenure, cultural fit, work satisfaction, and honesty. Perhaps one of the key points which limits the more extensive use of biodata is that it has to be developed for each organisation based on the criteria and biographical indicators linked to those criteria which surface for that organisation. A biodata developed for one group or one company cannot easily be transplanted to another and therefore proprietary models are almost impossible to develop. Furthermore, biodata cannot be built up from some general assumptions or pet notions; it has to be built from hard factual data, which necessitates a significant amount of 'investment' before any return can be made.

10

PSYCHOLOGICAL TESTING

Psychometrics

Psychological testing is one of the oldest, and perhaps most contentious, selection tools. As long ago as 500 BC, the Chinese were using a battery of psychological tests to aid the selection of government officials. Yet today they are still regarded by many as a new and unproved fad. Psychological tests are sometimes described as Psychometrics to denote that they are concerned with identifying the mental (psycho-) characteristics of people and putting a measurement (-metric) against such characteristics. Psychometric tests fall into two main types:

* ability tests
* personality tests.

Ability tests

Ability tests are sometimes known as aptitude tests and they are designed to simulate the work requirements so that a consistent sample of work is required to be undertaken by a range of candidates and their relative performance can then be measured.

A bricklayer being assessed for a job may be asked to lay a course of bricks as a means of demonstrating his or her competence. That would in its simplest sense be an ability test. In order to make meaningful comparisons between a range of applicants, however, it may be necessary to specify how many bricks are to be laid, in whatever pattern over a period of time.

There may be additional requirements or measures for the stability of the structure, wastage of materials, or the tidiness of the job. Furthermore, it may be necessary to establish that, for true comparison, it needs to be undertaken in the same weather conditions and therefore may become an indoor rather than an outdoor activity. In its crudest sense, therefore, laying the brick wall has become an ability test and by specifying the type of bricks, the number of courses to be laid, the pattern of laying and the timing etc – giving a standard set of instructions and a consistent environment – it should be possible to compare and contrast the performances of different bricklayers at different times in different places and by different testers in order to determine their relative abilities. This may tell us something about the candidates relative to each other but it may not necessarily tell us whether they would become proficient bricklayers, so a number of proficient bricklayers would be asked to undertake the test so that we can establish a comparative measure. This benchmark would be known as a normative sample and would perhaps say that they could lay x bricks in y minutes. For completeness it would be useful to have poor or incompetent bricklayers to complete the test so that we can identify the minimal amount of time in which the test is to be completed. This then becomes the normative data against which the candidates are measured to see whether or not they are up to the job. This is the simple and basic premise that underlies the development and application of ability tests. It is the attempt to identify whether someone has the ability to undertake the tasks for which they are being selected. It is therefore a test in the true sense of the word in that candidates may do well, do badly, or fail altogether.

A wide range of ability tests exist, including:

- typing tests based on work samples which ask candidates to type a set amount of text in a certain period of time
- tests of manual dexterity which would require operators to slot pegs into holes in a certain sequence and pattern over a period of time
- tests of spatial ability to see whether candidates are capable of operating machinery.

A driving test is probably the best known example of a widely used ability test.

There are some tests that are not based on work samples but are tests of an ability which is deemed to contribute to job performance. For example, tests of verbal skills, mental reasoning, and numeracy are common examples of tests used in clerical work situations. Some test are designed to identify the extent to which the individual is able to acquire and apply learning. These are called cognitive tests and work on the principle that job performance is a reflection of people's ability to acquire the knowledge needed to perform the job and apply that knowledge to new or unusual situations. An example of cognitive ability that is often used is that of a police officer dealing with crowds. Being taught the principles of crowd control is the skill to be learned but it will need to be applied in different situations; dealing with a crowd of onlookers at a car accident, dealing with a crowd of demonstrators where a protest demonstration is just getting out of hand, and dealing with a street crowd in the midst of an armed robbery are all aspects of crowd control, but police officers will be required to adapt their knowledge effectively to each of those situations. Cognitive tests attempt to identify this ability. Generally speaking, ability tests are divided into three main categories:

- *achievement tests*, which measure the knowledge and skill that the person has acquired. The tests mentioned above for bricklayers and typists would be seen as achievement tests. They are sometimes known as trade tests.

- *aptitude tests*, which may be based either on an occupational aptitude, such as computer programming or sales ability, or related to 'primary mental abilities' such as verbal reasoning, numerical ability, abstract reasoning, clerical speed and accuracy, mechanical reasoning, spatial ability, spelling and language usage. There are some tests which specifically measure one of the aptitudes, others which form a battery of measurements for a range of aptitudes and are known as 'differential aptitude batteries'.

- *intelligence tests*, which attempt to measure intelligence, albeit that there is some disagreement over the content of intelligence. In order to derive a measure of intelligence the tests may look at numerical aspects such as 'complete the missing number 2,4,7,11,..,22' or verbal aspects, posing questions such as 'man is to woman as bicycle is to . . .' (a spurious example, to which hard-line feminists will know the answer is 'fish').

There has been some argument over the value of intelligence tests. Until the 1980s they were not generally regarded as predictive of work performance, but a re-evaluation of research data in recent years has lead to a new movement in support for their use. It remains the case, however, that intelligence, however measured, is not a predictor of performance in high-level roles such as managerial positions. It has been argued that the popularity of IQ as a measure is a means of social discrimination (ensuring that class structures remain the determinant of workplace hierarchies, in the same vein that job evaluation reinforces and reflects wider class structures rather than economic and market forces on pay) rather than a determinant of potential performance. It is certainly the case that IQ tests discriminate against the under-privileged, which may potentially cause them to be indirect unlawful discrimination.

Personality tests

Although ability tests are tests in the true sense of levels of performance and of pass/fail, the same is not true of personality tests, which aim to gauge the innate traits and characteristics of people, codify them, and compare them with others'. In that sense the measures are comparisons rather than absolute values. Although ability tests have been in existence for several thousand years, personality tests are a more recent phenomenon and have existed for less than a century. They are an off-shoot of the development of intelligence tests, and there is still some blurring of boundaries between intelligence and personality in some of the tests that are marketed as personality tests. The greatest boost to development came in the 1940s with the requirement to select people for war duty, and to consider how different personalities would cope with different and extreme conditions. In particular, it was noted that fighter pilots could be in command of an aeroplane representing a substantial piece of investment, be taught to fly and be tested in that proficiency, but the moment of truth would come in aerial combat, so some process was needed for predicting whether the individual would be able to cope with such stress or would 'crack up'. It was thus in military usage that psychological testing became established, and it is still relied upon by many of the leading military forces in today's world. It is also interesting that the use of psychometric testing in World War II marked the cross-over of testing from clinical to occupational purposes. In the first half of the century, the focus of activity had been on psychological measurements in the context of mental ill health and mental illness. Many tests used psychiatric patients as their benchmark. World War I, of course, showed that the 'occupational' factor of soldiering could contribute to psychological damage – hence the attention to tests supplied to 'normal' people which would have hitherto been the domain of practitioners in clinics. Even beyond World War II, as occupational testing became more acceptable, many of the leading tests still held their origins or emphasis on clinical diagnosis rather than occupational guidance.

One of the most influential tests in the development of testing was the Minnesota Multiphasic Personality Inventory (MMPI). It was developed in the 1930s and measures nine separate psychiatric criteria. It has also been used for occupational testing purposes but because of its psychiatric connotations has been regarded as offensive. In the 1950s Cattell produced a theory of 16 factors constituting 'personality' and a test to measure those 16 factors called the 16PF. It became widely used and has probably been the single greatest influence on the development of occupational testing in the UK. One of the reasons for its popularity is the 'read-across' of personality factors into occupational suitability. There were, however, some questions that had a clinical 'feel' and made people apprehensive about its completion. The 16 factors used were:

cool – warm
concrete thinking – abstract thinking
affected by feelings – emotionally stable
submissive – dominant

sober – enthusiastic
expedient – conscientious
shy – bold
tough-minded – tender-minded
trusting – suspicious
practical – imaginative
forthright – shrewd
self-assured – apprehensive
conservative – experimenting
group oriented – self-sufficient
undisciplined/self conflict – following self-image
relaxed – tense

Of less popular note in the UK but of significant interest in the USA and in the world of testing generally has been the California Psychological Inventory (CPI) against which many occupational tests are benchmarked. The CPI measured 22 personality traits:

dominance
capacity for status
sociability
social presence
self-acceptance
sense of wellbeing (absence of worries)
responsibility
socialisation (social maturity/integrity)
self-control
tolerance
good impression (concerned with others' opinions)
communality
achievement via conformity
achievement via independence
intellectual efficiency
psychological mindedness
flexibility
femininity
empathy
independence
managerial potential
work orientation (strong work ethic)

The 16 PF and CPI, although used for occupational purposes such as selection, continue to be used for clinical diagnosis and counselling.

The importance of both the 16 PF and the CPI is that they attempt to sub-divide personality into distinguishable factors that are separate and describable. Although the tests are popular and effective, it has been difficult for others to correlate their research on personality with the 16 or 22 factors. In the 1930s McDougall wrote that 'personality may to advantage be broadly analysed into five distinguishable but separate factors, maybe intellect, character, temperament, disposition, and temper'. Researchers attempting to correlate their findings with the 16 PF and CPI found that there was more evidence of a smaller number, rather than greater number, of personality factors. In the 1950s Eysenck developed the theory that personality could be broken down into the 'big two' factors of extraversion and emotional stability, to support his theories on 'intelligence' (and was largely responsible for popularising the myth that extraversion is a prerequisite of high performance). Eysenck was particularly successful at predicting pilot suitability through his work. In the 1960s a number of studies served to support the view that personality could be divided into five factors. One study by Borgatta was significant in that five stable factors were defined through five different methods of data gathering. Another study by Norman labelled the factors:

- extroversion
- emotional stability
- agreeableness
- conscientiousness
- culture (more recently labelled 'intellectance' or 'openness to experience')

These have come to be known as the 'Big Five'. In the 1970s, 1980s and 1990s, numerous studies have served to reinforce the validity of the big five. In 1987 McCrae and Costa published research, followed in 1991 by Barrick and Mount, into meta-analysis of studies of the big five and predictions of job performance, measured against such aspects as productivity, tenure, status change, salary, performance rating. The study showed that the big five factors were valid predictors of work performance and that one factor in particular, 'conscientiousness', was a particularly effective predictor of all aspects of job performance.

The five factors cover aspects of human nature reflecting:

- traits such as being gregarious, assertive, talkative and active, together with ambition, expressiveness and impetuousness (extroversion/introversion)
- aspects such as anxiety, anger, worry, insecurity, together with resilience and independent thought (emotional stability)
- social conformity, being courteous, flexible, co-operative, forgiving, soft-hearted, tolerant, trusting or cynical (agreeableness – sometimes also labelled 'likeability')
- hard-working, persevering, careful, organised, and preferences for rules and procedures or spontaneity and creativity (conscientiousness)
- curious, imaginative, broad-minded traits as well as 'intelligence' – however defined (openness to experience).

It is important to realise that none of the personality factors are in themselves good or bad, or have good or bad ends to their scales, merely differences which make some personalities more suitable for certain activities than others. The combination of factors is a very important consideration. For example, someone high on extroversion and low in another factor such as agreeableness will act very differently from someone also high on extroversion but high on agreeableness; the volume and mix determines the final cocktail. It may seem uncomfortable to divide the vast range of personalities into five criteria but they are five sub-sections rather than five types. In the same way that the six balls in the National Lottery create imponderable permutations, so too do the permutations of the five factors create the rich tapestry of human behaviour.

The emergence of the big five theory has enabled psychologists to develop occupational tests concerned with predicting job performance and used purely for selection rather than spin-offs from clinical diagnosis. This has enabled tests to be developed without using contentious questions such as 'Do you feel suicidal?' and has made them more acceptable to candidates as part of the selection process. In the UK, the emergence of a small number of active and highly visible test developers and suppliers, committed to energetic marketing, has served to increase the acceptability, usage and reliability of occupational tests. This does *not* mean that they are infallible or totally objective, as Table 10 shows, so purchasers should always proceed with care.

Test quality and choice

To ensure that tests are able to do the things that they claim to do, some standards of quality are applied. These standards are concerned with the validity and reliability of tests.

Table 10
TESTS AND HOROSCOPES

Tests are often said to be objective. They are not. They simply absorb the test-takers' views of themselves, record them, codify and regurgitate them in a set of standard responses. In that sense, therefore, they are not a 'black box' but a process similar to an interview, if less transparent and more controlled. Research has shown that people's self-perception as evidenced by test results is remarkably consistent and impartial. Test publishers often sell their tests by asking the purchaser to sample, and offer the opportunity to provide a test result on the purchaser. Who, after all, is best able to assess the description of the purchaser than the purchaser? The purchaser then completes the test and, surprise surprise, is provided with an 'uncannily accurate picture' of themselves. A good test will do this, but a nonsense test with a carefully crafted narrative will do the same. Take, for example, the statement 'you feel less comfortable making decisions and resolving problems in the absence of feedback from your boss'. Such a narrative is likely to lead to nodding heads and sageful sighs if given in response to the personality test for most managers in today's climate. A psychologist charted such an effect by asking a conference of human resource managers to complete a (valid) psychometric test and, instead of providing the proper result, gave them bogus feedback in the form of 13 statements taken from horoscopes. When asked about the accuracy, none of the test-takers thought the results were wrong, 40 per cent thought them 'rather good' and over 50 per cent viewed them as 'amazingly accurate'. Unscrupulous test publishers will ensure that their narrative is suitably vague and horoscope-like to make the test results acceptable. A good test will give the test-taker feedback that includes information that gives 'a glow', together with some uncomfortable 'home truths'.

Validity

Validity is expressed in different ways:

- face validity
- content validity
- construct validity
- criterion related validity.

Face validity is concerned with the question 'Does the test appear to measure what it is supposed to measure?'. This depends on the nature of the test and the context in which it would be used. Face validity is concerned with people's perceptions of what a test measures, therefore it is not a true kind of validity, and is usually played down by psychologists, but it is of great practical importance for selectors wishing to avoid giving offence to candidates and being ridiculed by line colleagues.

Content validity relates to the question 'Do the items in the test adequately cover every aspect of what the test is supposed to measure?'. If, for example, the 'analytical reasoning' was identified as a test subject and defined as a general mental ability involving both numerical and verbal components, any test designed to measure 'analytical reasoning' would need to include both numerical and verbal items; the absence of either one would reduce the content validity of the test.

Construct validity is theoretically the most interesting type because it relates to the issue of whether the idea behind the test is valid or not. For practical purposes it is concerned with the question 'Does the test really measure what it is supposed to measure and not something else?'. If, for example, we established a test for a sixth dimension of personality, then we would need to demonstrate that this additional sixth dimension was real and that the test measured it, rather than measuring one of the big five and naming it in a different way. Equally, if the test is supposed to be measuring full personality then it will need to be seen to be measuring all five factors, not just some of them. Most modern occupational tests are constructed on the basis of the big five and therefore the focus of attention is usually on the effectiveness of the test in measuring those dimensions, rather than on the theory behind the test.

Criterion-related validity has the most practical significance for selectors as it is concerned with the question 'Do the scores on the test relate to anything important in the world of work?'. In occupational testing 'anything important' is usually some measure of job performance such as supervisors' ratings, sales achieved, absence, turnover or achievement.

Reliability

Reliability is looked at in three ways:

- test – retest reliability
- internal consistency
- parallel forms reliability.

Test-retest is concerned with the stability of test scores over time. It involves administering the test to the same individuals on two or more separate occasions, normally a few weeks or months apart. The test-retest reliability is for correlation between the scores obtained on the two occasions. Although in theory there is concern about rehearsing people by retaking tests, in practice the results of the two or more occasions will need to be consistent, because different results will tend to show that it is the test that is inconsistent rather than the people taking it.

Internal consistency is concerned with the idea that all of the items within a test should be measuring the same thing and therefore should be correlated with each other. For example, if a test question asked 'Do you prefer going to parties or learning a new skill?', it would be an inconsistent question because the first part of the question will be linked to 'extraversion' and the second part of the question will be linked to 'openness to experience'.

Parallel forms reliability is the ability of a test to measure in the same way as another test designed to measure the same construct. It is particularly important if the publishers produces two versions of the same test, since they should then be highly correlated.

Reliability and validity are both important in deciding whether a test is of sufficient quality. Reliability, however, is generally more important than validity since a test cannot measure anything at all if it does not at least measure it consistently. Measures are usually expressed as a 'correlation coefficient'. This is an index of the strength of the relationship between two variables (for example, the test result and a supervisor's rating) which varies from a 'perfect negative relationship' of –1 (as the test scores go up, the supervisor's rating scores go down), through 'no relationship' of 0, to a 'perfect positive relationship' of +1 (scores for the test and supervisor's rating go up and down together). Generally speaking, 0.7 is regarded as the minimum score for reliability and 0.3 is regarded as useful for criterion-related validity.

Quality is, of course, defined as meeting the specification. One of the difficulties faced when looking for suitable tests is being clear about what it is to be used for. To say a Rolls-Royce is a good car is not a point of argument, but if the car needed is a cheap run-around that is easy to park then it is not particularly suitable. There is a great danger in being coaxed into buying tests from test publishers because they have been proven as suitable for a particular organisation when the real starting point ought to be the recruiter's own organisation's needs. The first stage should therefore be determining what it is that the test is going to measure. Using the competency framework outlined in Chapter 5,

- competencies that fall under the acquired or performing clusters would lend themselves to ability testing
- competencies falling under the natural and adapting clusters would lend themselves to personality testing.

In looking at the overall selection process, it is also worth considering whether other techniques would be more suitable than the selection test. For the 'performing' cluster, assessment centre and work sampling would be appropriate. For the 'acquired' cluster, the evidence of educational certificates or professional qualifications or appropriate experience could be gained through the application form or biodata. The competencies in the 'performing' and 'adapting' clusters could also be probed through interview as could some of the competencies in the 'natural' cluster. It is, however, in the 'natural' cluster that testing will offer an advantage over other techniques. Many personality characteristics are subtle nuances rather than stereotypes. In adulthood, most people have learned to acquire behaviours which mask or enhance, as appropriate, their personality dimensions. Observation and interview may not reveal the hidden depths. There are, for example, many cases of film stars and musicians whose ebullient and charismatic public persona masked an anxious and introverted personality. In such cases the sad price of career achievement is the high cost of personal failure and perhaps reliance on alcohol or drugs. So, too, in the workplace it may be difficult accurately to gauge the personality and probable behaviours of people without the use of personality testing. It is highly unlikely that Barings Bank used personality testing for selection of its dealers and management, since it would have helped avert its collapse.

Before using a test we therefore need to be quite clear what it is we are testing for. This is equally important whether choosing an ability test or a personality test. There have been high-profile discrimination cases in the UK in recent years concerning the use of testing, and these have usually been ability tests. One notable case was that of train drivers being required to undergo a test that measured their competence in the English language. The case was settled before being heard, but the argument was made that language proficiency was unrelated to the skill of driving a railway engine; it was directly discriminatory against those whose first language was not English.

Choices

The two approaches for choosing tests are the rational approach and the empirical approach. The rational approach is to undertake an analysis of the person-requirements, preferably using a competencies approach, based on role analysis. This identifies the key criteria to be tested. The next stage is to identify tests which will accurately measure such criteria.

The empirical approach is to pilot a large battery of tests on the existing population and undertake a statistical correlation with factors of job performance. This will identify the key criteria or competencies and, simultaneously, show which test is most appropriate for identifying them. Further guidance on these approaches is contained in the chapter on role analysis (Chapter 6).

Whichever approach is used, it is important to ensure good-quality advice, and if an organisation does not have a psychologist in-house then the services of an independent psychologist would be a worthwhile investment. Reliance on test publishers' recommendations or the suitability of the test for other organisations is a risky approach.

In choosing a test, selectors may decide to:

- buy a proprietary test
- adopt a free test
- develop their own test.

The most popular approach is to buy proprietary tests. This may be due in part to the fact that much of the growth in test usage in the UK is attributable to the marketing efforts of test publishers. In general, buying a proprietary test means that the hard work of development has already been undertaken, there will usually be a good level of support for further development and copies of the test and other materials, validation studies will have been undertaken correctly, and proper training and technical support will be available. These are the advantages that would accrue from buying a proprietary test but they do not necessarily flow in all cases

Table 11
CHOOSING A TEST

- Be clear on why the test is needed and what it is going to measure.
- Look for evidence of reliability (0.70 or greater).
- Look for evidence of validity (0.3 or greater)
    - for a personality test, is it based on the big-5 factors?
    - does it predict job performance?
- Expect to see a manual giving all the above data, plus development background and administration instructions.
- Confirm the availability of benchmark comparisons (normative data).
- Ensure the test is not discriminatory in design or application.
- Check availability of training and support.
- Clarify cost arrangements and any hidden 'licence fees' etc.
- See whether it is used elsewhere, but avoid
    - taking other's views on its suitability for you
    - an over-used test that your candidates may not be new to.

and all these selling points should be checked.

Using a free test may seem an option too good to be true. There are, however, thousands of tests available which have been developed by researchers as part of wider studies, perhaps on theories of personality type. It is often the case that such researchers do not want their academic rigour sullied by commercial consideration, and their lack of entrepreneurial opportunism should not therefore be regarded as any lack of faith in their own test. It is also the case that very often such tests have much greater evidence of validity and reliability studies than proprietary tests, where commercial pressures may have necessitated some short cuts in development. The great advantage of the tests is that they carry no fees for use, no licence charges, and no obligation to undertake supplier training. The downside is that training will be unlikely to be available, technical support will not be forthcoming and no reliance can be made on any further developments. There is also a greater opportunity (but usually no greater likelihood) that candidates will be able to also get hold of the test beforehand.

The third option is 'Do-It-Yourself ' test development. This is feasible and has the advantage that it can be geared specifically to the needs of the organisation, and that control of costs, further development, training and support are all within the organisation's domain. The time and cost of development, however, are likely to be significant and, where the organisation does not have its own psychologists, will mean sub-contracting the development to external psychologists, which means reliance on the third party for further development, training, support, etc. Where, however, there is likely to be a large-scale recruitment activity over a sustained period, it may be far more cost-effective for the organisation to undertake this approach than to buy-in proprietary tests. General guidelines for choosing tests appear in Table 11.

Test appearance

Ability tests
Ability tests look like the tests that most people would have encountered in childhood, although the ability being tested

will dictate the final appearance of the test. An example appears in Table 12. Ability tests are often 'power' tests, which means that it is highly unlikely that test takers will be able to complete the test within the period allocated. Results are driven by the speed of the test taker and the accuracy of the answers. Because they are tests in the strict sense of the word, test conditions need to be applied and specific instructions are given to candidates, the timing carefully controlled through the use of a stopwatch, and 'examination room' conditions set up. The tests will usually be supplied with a scoring key, frequently in the form of a template, which is often computerised. The scores are compared with the scores of the benchmark population (referred to as the 'population norm'), to determine whether the results are high, low etc. The population norm is usually the group which the test publisher used in developing the test; these are invariably schoolchildren or university students. This can be a particular problem for placing reliance on some ability tests where such test-takers will generally be more 'rehearsed' through their environment and therefore more adept than an older working population.

Table 12
AN EXAMPLE OF AN ABILITY TEST

Below is a handwritten list. A typed version of the list is shown in the **shaded answer box.** In the typed version the names have been re-ordered alphabetically by surname. Ring the errors in the **typed list.**

Handwritten list	Typed list
S. Hodges	Bailey H. E.
P. J. Levett	Briscombe G.
W. W. Robinson	Cooper L.S.
G. L. Briscombe	Fitzsimons A. P.
A. P. Fitzsimmons	Hodges S.
D. M. Overfield	Levet P. J.
L. S. Cooper	Overfield D. J.
H. E. Bailey	Robinson W. W.

Extract from the Modern Occupational Skills Test, reproduced with the permission of ASE Test Publishing.

Personality tests

Personality tests do not look like tests as such; they are really questionnaires. They usually, but not always, take the form of:

- statements
- choices
- adjectives.

The 'statement' type are usually open-ended questions to which the candidate replies 'true' or 'false' or may have a range of responses from 'very much like me' to 'not at all like me', or similar descriptions. (An extract from one appears in Table 13.) These tests are usually constructed in such a way that the question will be asked in many different ways on a number of occasions as a means of gauging a typical answer. In an omnibus test (full personality) this means the test may cover over a hundred questions.

The 'choice' type, sometimes called ipsative, is one in which the test taker is required to make a choice between two statements or adjectives. Sometimes it is a straight choice; sometimes there is a scale of response. There is some concern about the use of such tests. To illustrate, if we provide a test taker with a choice 'I often beat my spouse and family' or 'I often steal from shops or my employer' we will be able to

Table 13
EXTRACT FROM A PERSONALITY TEST

Please read each question; then, on the answer sheet, shade T for True or F for False, whichever is appropriate to you. Please be as honest as you can in your answers.

1. I have no particular desire to be the leader of a group.	T	F
2. I shy away from situations where I might be asked to take charge.	T	F
3. I let others take the lead when I'm on a committee.	T	F
4. I would avoid a job which required me to supervise other people.	T	F
5. I work best in a group when I'm the person in charge.	T	F

Extracted from the Assertiveness Style Questionnaire, developed by M. Lorr and W. More.

deduce from the answer that the test taker either has violent tendencies or dishonest tendencies. In practice the respondent could be either violent or dishonest or both or neither. Deducing answers from forced choices is therefore fraught with difficulties. Nevertheless, it remains a feature of some dubious tests – but also of some very valid and well-constructed tests.

The 'adjective' test has become more popular in recent years, partly because of improvements in its development and partly because it generally offers a quicker and more cost-effective route to testing. In this approach test takers are required to respond to an adjective as 'like me' or 'not like me' etc or respond to a choice of adjectives indicating which is most appropriate for them. An extract from one appears in Table 14.

Table 14
EXTRACT FROM AN ADJECTIVE TEST

Instructions

1. This questionnaire contains a list of common trait adjectives which describe how people behave and feel.
2. Please indicate how far each adjective describes your typical behaviour using the scale below.
3. Mark the scale with a tick, circle or cross. Use a ball-point pen and press hard.
4. Please complete all the items.

Rating scale

a   Very
b   Quite
c   Moderately
d   Slightly
e   Not at all

Please describe your typical behaviour using the following adjectives:

1 **Curious**	a	b	c	d	e	2 **Agreeable**	a	b	c	d	e
3 **Careful**	a	b	c	d	e	4 **Active**	a	b	c	d	e
5 **Stable**	a	b	c	d	e	6 **Conservative**	a	b	c	d	e
7 **Uncaring**	a	b	c	d	e	8 **Disorganised**	a	b	c	d	e
9 **Restrained**	a	b	c	d	e	10 **Anxious**	a	b	c	d	e

Extracted from the MPQ test, reproduced with the
permission of CIM Test Publishing.

Whatever the style of the personality test, it is not a test in the strict sense, and therefore timing is not important other than in keeping to the schedule of the selector. There is often a guide schedule and this will vary, according to the test, from 15 minutes to 90 minutes or more. It is often the case that personality tests are available in either paper-and-pencil format or on computer screen. It is also the norm nowadays for the test results to be calculated by the computer and output produced either as a set of raw scores, or a set of sten scores (a standard ten-point scale derived from the range of responses in the population norm) and often with a narrative report which is derived from logarithms of test results and candidate profiles. An example of feedback on a single competency from an MPQ Personality Assessment appears in Table 15. Although personality tests are not strictly tests it is usually the case, however, that administration is undertaken in test examination conditions.

Table 15
EXTRACT FROM A PERSONALITY ASSESSMENT REPORT

Information and decision-making

A competent decision-maker gets and uses information, identifies ideas and finds ways of using them, and makes use of situations.

He tends to make decisions in the following way:

- Because he is fairly impulsive, his ability to make rational decisions based on analysis of relevant facts and information is less developed than in most people (S9–).
- He is as likely as most to involve others and make decisions that show consideration for people's values and situations (S6).
- He is as open to new ideas and approaches as the average person when making decisions (S3).
- He is extremely willing to take risks and break rules when making decisions (S2+).
- He is a fairly innovative person who comes up with ideas, finds ways of using them and makes creative decisions (S1+).
- He feels in control of things and is ready to act when the situation requires it (S13+).

Reproduced with the permission of CIM Test Publishing.

Administration

The use and administration of psychological tests in the UK is carefully controlled. The British Psychological Society grants a licence to undertake the administration and scoring of ability tests (level A) and the administration, scoring and interpretation of personality tests (level B). The level A qualification is a prerequisite of level B training. Training is provided by psychologists, approved by the BPS. In many cases the test publishers provide the training. Test publishers restrict supplies of tests to licensed people (individuals, not organisations). The costs of training are substantial; approximately six days of training for each level. Although publishers provide general training at level B, it is often the case that they require users to undertake further specific training in their own tests. There is some concern over whether the licence system is a safety precaution or a closed shop. Given the opportunity to apply computer-based administration, scoring, interpretation and report-generation, the on-going validity of the current approach is subject to question.

11

INTERVIEWING

Popularity

The interview is the most popular selection technique. It is the most popular in two senses; it is the technique most frequently used in selection decisions and it is the technique upon which most reliance is placed in formulating the selection decision. It can also be one of the least effective and most ill-used of selection tools.

Recent studies in the UK, by the Institute of Employment Studies, Industrial Relations Services and Hays Accounting, have shown that the interview is used in more than 90 per cent of selection assignments. This is not a UK phenomenon particularly – the same conclusions arise from studies in various countries around the world. It is also popular from a candidate's viewpoint; if the first aspiration of candidates is to get the job then the second is certainly to get an interview. A selection decision made without any interview taking place will be one viewed by candidates with suspicion, if not hostility. It is, of course, one of the few parts of the selection process, and one of the few techniques, which is truly a two-way process. The reason for the popularity of interviews may be the fact that it is a very natural process; being able to sit and talk to others is a skill which is not confined to the professional recruiter and is shared by the candidate and the line manager or client. It may also be a cause of the downfall of many interviews which are designed as an opportunity to talk rather than a technique for gathering data on a candidate in order to make a decision. Even in the most sophisticated selection assignments, it can nevertheless be the case that candidates are called to a number of interviews, sometimes even with the same interviewer. The IRS study in 1996 revealed that one in six employers asked managerial candidates to face three or more interviews. This casts serious doubt on the efficacy of the first two interviews and the decision-making ability of the selectors. This is perhaps both the crux of the problem with interviews and the centre of opportunity. The interview can be a very effective technique if properly focused, used and analysed.

Uses

The interview is a versatile tool which can be used for a number of purposes.

Information exchange

One purpose is to enable the candidate to find out more about the role, about the organisation, and other factors which will be important in helping the candidate to make a decision whether to apply to the organisation or accept the job. In a scarce labour market, where there are many organisations chasing a few candidates, certain kinds of interview can be an effective technique for 'hooking' candidates and helping them to make decisions about the organisation based on a feel for it and its people without having to make hard decisions based on brochures or other impersonal data. It can therefore serve as an attracting process, and one in which the preparation of the selector is geared more to responding to candidates' potential questions than preparing questions to ask the candidate. Although not interviewing the candidate overtly, the selector should nevertheless be in a position to apply subtle techniques of gathering data from the candidate so that a two-way interview is taking place. Many 'open days', career fairs and trade shows are therefore opportunities for interviews to take place. Similarly, even the humble job vacancy notice in the shop window provides an opportunity for an interview to take place when potential candidates make an enquiry, even if that enquiry is simply asking for an application form.

Screening

The second use of an interview may be for screening purposes. Although it is a costly technique, in that it takes the valuable resource of selectors to undertake, it can be very effective particularly if there is not a very large volume of response in the first place. A short 10- to 15-minute interview can cover more than sufficient information to make decisions on whether to proceed with the candidate's application. It has the advantage of the personal touch and provides the opportunity to give information to candidates about the organisation, and a 'feel' for whether they wish to continue with their application. Using the interview as a screening process needs to be a clear decision, however, and not by default. Some organisations ask candidates to complete an application form and proceed to a 'first interview' without taking more than a cursory glance at the application form. In such circumstances it is better to decide whether to place reliance on the form for screening or disregard the form and use the interview as a screening process. Being half-hearted about both means being productive on neither.

Selection

The third use of interviewing is for selection decisions, which may be undertaken in tandem with other techniques, such as testing or assessment exercises, or as the sole decision point. Using the interview as the final selection tool requires a greater degree of sophistication and preparation but it remains the case that whatever use is made of the interview it will be more effective if it is properly prepared, has a clear focus, and is undertaken by skilled people. There has been criticism of the interview as an effective selection technique but much of the criticism has been about the way in which it has been used rather than the technique itself. A junior member of staff sitting down with a candidate for an unprepared 'chat' and without being given a clear specification for the job being sought, or time to research the candidate's biography, may not yield a particularly good result but this is more of a reflection on the selector than it is on the value of the interview process itself. It is the case that all too often the interview has been criticised as an ineffective technique when it is the people undertaking it and the circumstances in which it is undertaken that is at fault.

Interview panels

There is no golden rule about the appropriate number of interviewers for an interview; it is a matter of organisational preference. Research does not prove conclusively that panel interviews are *per se* more effective than one-to-one interviews. Some organisations prefer to have a series of one-to-one interviews, others prefer to use a panel approach, some more formal than others. It is the usual practice for search and selection consultants to undertake a one-to-one interview to prepare a shortlist which is then submitted to the client for final interview.

The modern practice inclines towards an interviewing duo. This consists of a skilled interviewer, usually a member of the HR department, and the 'client', ie the person who has requested the selection process and for whom the successful candidate will be working directly or ultimately. The importance of involving the client cannot be over-emphasised. However objective the interview and other selection tools may be, it remains an important element in selection that the chemistry between the new hire and his or her boss is right. This is a two-way process and it is as much in the interest of the candidate as in the interest of the organisation. There are many cases where a technically sound appointment has gone wrong and the new hire has failed to optimise his or her contribution simply because of a personality difference. This is a simple fact of working life and it is important that the selection process recognises it. It is also the case that however effective the techniques are, and however sound the decision may be, selecting people is still a very personal issue and it is all too easy for clients to criticise the selectors for their decision. Agreeing a clear specification is one of the most important ways of avoiding this problem but equally, involving the client-manager in the decision and judgement is also important.

Although there is no golden rule on the number of interviewers, it is obvious that it needs to be a small enough number to facilitate decision-making and avoid intimidating the candidate. Some organisations have engaged in some absurd practices, notably some local authorities which involve the full Council in the selection interview. This may be useful as an opportunity for the candidate to undertake a selling presentation but it is stretching the point to call it an interview.

The composition of the interview panel will depend upon the purpose of the interview. An interview designed to investigate personal qualities can be undertaken by any skilled interviewer without detailed knowledge of the work that the candidate will be performing. An interview designed to investigate technical capability or experience will, of course, necessitate someone with such knowledge and expertise in order to judge the response. There may be occasions where a regulatory requirement exists for an independent assessor to be present or for a particular specialist; this is particularly the case in many NHS professional appointments. In organisations where teamworking is of great importance it may be appropriate to involve peers in the process of selection. There is an academic argument which supports the notion that subordinates should be involved in the selection of their boss (because effective leadership is determined by the acceptance of the group being lead) but there are very few reported examples of this, although the use of 360-degree assessment as a selection tool is gaining popularity in the USA.

Types

The main types of interview are:

- unstructured
- structured.

Unstructured interviews

Unstructured interviews follow a natural process of dialogue and, although unstructured, may involve the interviewer in asking some 'favourite' questions. The unstructured interview may also pose some questions around the application form or CV, or a set of questions around aspects such as work history, aspirations, personal circumstances etc. It is unstructured in the sense that the candidate is encouraged to lead the interview and talk freely in response to the set of questions or even to just one opening question. The advantage of the unstructured interview is that candidates may feel more comfortable with the process and are able to cover those aspects which they would wish to see covered. It also enables the interviewer to concentrate on listening, recording and assessing the response. Some unstructured interviews take the form of an informal dialogue but again with the interviewer placing less reliance on framing the question and more on listening to the answers. A further 'advantage' of the unstructured interview is that it requires little in the way of preparation, particularly in terms of reviewing the application or CV. The disadvantages of the unstructured interview are that it relies heavily on the ability of the interviewer, particularly in terms of assessment skills; it is inconsistent and provides little basis for comparison between candidates; is difficult to control, particularly the time element; and it is generally less effective than a structured interview. All research has shown that structured interviews are significantly more effective than unstructured interviews.

Structured interviews

Structured interviews, although more effective, are generally less common. They fall into two main types:

- situational interviews
- behavioural interviews.

In simple terms the difference between the two is that the situational interview asks the candidate to put him or herself into some hypothetical situation and describe how they would handle it, whereas in the behavioural interview the candidate is asked to recall specific examples from their past experience and describe what they did. Research has shown that the behavioural interview is more effective than the situational interview and is less likely to lead to unfair discrimination, but both types are far more effective than unstructured interviews.

The *situational interview* is almost like a verbal role play. The candidate is presented with a potential future scenario and asked how they would be likely to handle it. For example, an interviewee for a supervisory position in a packaging department may be asked:

> 'You are at the start of the day's operations, a third of your shift has failed to appear because of a flu epidemic, you have two lines of product which need to be packed today. Product A is the company's main product and is particularly profitable. Product B is a new product on which the company is still recovering development costs. The reduced labour availability means you will not be able to meet the targets for packaging both product A and product B. All the product and packing materials for product B have been delivered to your packing hall, the product and inner boxes for product A have been delivered but not the outer boxes into which the inner boxes have to be packed. What do you do next?'

Such a question may be designed to assess how the candidate will cope with pressure, how they will undertake their planning and organising, or how they will approach problem-solving. The benefit of this kind of situational interview is that it is work-related, it provides the candidate with a flavour of the kinds of things with which they will be faced, it focuses judgement on work-related rather than peripheral or abstract qualities, and it is often welcomed by the candidate as a more thorough and realistic interview than a general unstructured 'chit-chat'.

The *behavioural interview* works on the premise that the best indicator of future behaviour is past behaviour; and that the way in which a person responded to a situation in the past is the most likely indication of how they will respond in the future. The situational interview may indicate that the candidate knows how to handle a particular situation but knowing what to do doesn't necessarily indicate the propensity to do it when the time comes. The behavioural interview is, however, focused on the behaviours or competencies which underpin job performance. Interview questions are then framed with a view to eliciting information about those behaviours or competencies. The question is, of course, only an opening question and enables the interviewer to probe the responses of the interviewee. The question is framed with reference to the candidate's own history so that the example can be anchored in past history rather than future speculation.

Thus, taking the example above, seeking to assess the problem-solving capabilities of the candidate for the packaging supervisor position, the interviewer may ask the question:

'What's the most difficult problem you've encountered in the last six months in your role?'

The same question could be adapted to school life, home life, studies, hobbies etc. The candidate is allowed to provide examples of past behaviour that will give an indication of their future behaviour. Thus the candidate may answer:

'Dealing with the insurance claims for lost luggage of people while they were still on holiday.'

Note that this has nothing to do with working in a packing hall. Yet it is an opportunity to explore problem-solving in an entirely different context but which will reveal the problem-solving capabilities of the candidate that they would be likely to apply in the role of supervisor in the packaging department. The answer above is, of course, too superficial to facilitate judgement. In order to assess the behaviour it would be necessary for the interviewer to further explore the answer and he or she would ask for a specific recent example and then start to probe through detailed follow-up questions. This provides concrete examples and the interviewer would then be in a position to assess whether the candidate was proficient or not in their past attempts at problem-solving. The past success or failure would provide a reliable indication of their effectiveness at future problem-solving.

The use of a competency-based approach to selection permits the structured behavioural interview technique to be adopted, allowing the interviewer to structure questions around the key competencies identified for the role. This provides a clear focus for the interview and allows a consistent approach for interviewers to adopt, so that if different interviewers are engaged in the process they can distribute the interviewing tasks effectively by each concentrating on different competencies or where perhaps the recruiter and the client are interviewing separately on the same competency, they have a common basis on which to compare the response. Furthermore the competency framework will usually include descriptions of behaviours of the competency in action in everyday use. These can act as a guide to identify 'good' or 'poor' answers. It is often the case that interviewers know how to frame the question but may have more difficulty in evaluating the answers given and determining whether they are demonstrating the required level of ability, or a higher or lower level. Research has shown that using behavioural examples of the competencies as a guide to evaluating candidates' answers, increases the efficiency of the interview process. In practical terms it is also a very welcome benefit for clients and colleagues who may be involved in recruitment as an adjunct to, rather than the mainstream of, their work.

A well-constructed, behaviourally based structured interview will enable an interviewer to explore four to six competencies in a period of about 45 minutes, or fewer for a well-skilled interviewer. This is a particularly efficient use of interview time and, since it is focused on a certain number of competencies, means that attention is paid to using other techniques to measure the other competencies thereby making an efficient use of the overall selection process rather than duplicating interviews with screening and testing etc and attempting to reconcile a hotch-potch of information.

Choice

There are advantages and disadvantages to the various types of interview.

The unstructured interview can be undertaken with a minimum of training, requires less preparation, and allows candidates a great degree of flexibility. The disadvantages are that it is less effective at predicting performance than structured interviews, it can be uncomfortable for occasional interviewers such as line colleagues or clients, and is difficult to compartmentalise into an overall selection process. The lack of compartmentalisation often means that interview assessments are inconsistent between candidates, and can be at odds with other parts of the selection process, such as testing. It is often the case that different interviewers reach different conclusions about the candidate, and often over non-specific generalisations.

The advantage of the structured interview, whether situational or behavioural, is that it is a more effective predictor of performance than the unstructured interview. In general, structured interviews are better perceived by candidates who feel that the interview has been relevant and thorough. The focus also makes it easier to prepare meaningful reports on candidates. The disadvantage of the structured interview is that it is not a natural process and requires training and experience to raise the skill of the interviewer. A particular disadvantage of the situational interview is that it has the potential to be discriminatory, since it requires candidates to hypothesise about future situations and use indirect formal language in an unfamiliar artificial context. For ethnic minority applicants whose first language may not be English, this may create a disadvantage. It may also make the interview unnecessarily difficult for people working in a shop-floor environment where a more direct and colourful language may be the norm. There is the danger, therefore, that the interviews are more a test of English language than an investigation into the particular competency. The behavioural interview does not suffer from this disadvantage and, indeed, has the added advantage that transporting people back to their past experiences, and asking them to talk about it, makes it much easier for them to answer the questions by relating to specific issues.

Interviewing principles

Interviewing is not a natural activity. Successful interviewing is a task requiring the application of skill and planning. It is not unusual for an interviewer to be as nervous as the candidate, particularly where the interviewer is new to the experience. Even experienced interviewers sometime suffer some of the downsides – the inability to keep from making a snap judgement in the first few minutes, trying to control candidates, maintaining concentration in the middle part of the interview, remembering all the candidates who are interviewed . . . the list goes on. Yet a good interview is not too difficult to conduct; it can be pleasant, meaningful, and need not take more than 30 minutes to provide sound data on which to make a good judgement, particularly where it is used as part of an overall selection process involving other techniques. Following some key principles and adopting them as good habits will help to improve interviewing effectiveness.

Prepare

Before the interview the interviewer should ensure that he or she is fully prepared to conduct the interview and that all arrangements have been made to present a professional image to the candidate. This involves a thorough reading of the application form, making sure there will be no interruptions during the interview, and preparing the interview questions.

Welcome

A proper welcome creates the right atmosphere for mutual confidence throughout the interview. The relationship between the candidate and the interviewer should be friendly, supportive and non-threatening. By building a rapport and putting the candidate at ease the interviewer will be more likely to get spontaneous, and therefore honest, answers to questions. Care needs to be taken with the interview surroundings. It is, sadly, not unusual to find 'confidential' interviews being undertaken in the midst of a busy hotel lounge with hapless candidates balancing coffee and papers while attempting to answer questions in a confident and up-beat way without the conversation being overheard by others in the lounge – many of whom are nonchalantly drinking their coffee and straining to hear every word. The most effective interviewing environment is a quiet office, with telephones diverted and interruptions barred, and with seating in a semi-formal arrangement.

Control

Most interviews are designed to last a scheduled time. The interviewer will need to ensure that information on the key criteria is collected in that time. It is important that the interviewer maintains control of the interview and may need to encourage reticent candidates to provide more detail in their answers, or restrict the output of more garrulous candidates. Candidates need cues to help them know what is expected. Some interviews that they have attended may have consisted of only one question and they were expected to keep the rest of the interview going; others may have been a continuous stream of investigative questions. It is important, therefore, to help the candidate understand how the interview will be structured, that there will be time for the candidate to ask questions, either at the beginning or the end, and that the interviewer will ask one question, several questions, or whatever. In maintaining control it is important that the candidate is treated properly and allowed to maintain self-esteem and confidence.

Probe

The purpose of an interview is to gain evidence to show whether the candidate does or does not have the appropriate qualities to undertake the role. Interviewers must therefore expect to go beyond the platitudes and find real answers and be prepared to 'interrogate', but in a way that does not seem overtly intrusive. During the interview it is possible to keep the candidate focused on the right issue by using certain questioning techniques. Interviewers should ask simple open-ended questions, trying to avoid leading the candidate or suggesting the answer required. Examples may be 'How do you organise your work?' or 'What sort of problem did you have to tackle?'. The questions should be indirect, using phrases such as 'how, when, where, why, who, what, which, tell me more, in what way, explain, describe'. Indirect and open-ended questions will generally yield a better response from candidates. Direct questions and closed questions will be less productive. A direct question will invite a yes or no response and close down the dialogue. For example, asking the question 'How is your health?' will almost certainly produce the reply 'Good'. Asking specifically 'How much sickness absence have you taken in the last six months?' or 'When was your most recent illness?' will lead to an answer which is capable of being explored further. Similarly, leading questions are to be avoided. Asking 'I imagine you are accomplished at delegating?' will have a predictable answer.

Clarify

It is important to pin down specific examples in the candidate's answers if they are to be relied upon. All too often interviewers will be pleased to receive an answer and move to the next question even though that answer does not provide the information required. Very often, interview questions need to be followed up with several probing questions before the required information is provided with sufficient clarity. It is also important to seek balanced information – searching for 'contrary evidence'. In the event that the candidate provides an answer that appears to demonstrate that they have high levels of problem-solving ability, the interviewer should pose questions aimed at uncovering any difficulties with problem-solving. The interviewer should then be able to assess the frequency or severity of poor problem-solving and hence gauge the candidate's ability in this regard.

Notes

No one has a perfect memory and note-taking is therefore important. Taking notes is not easy and needs practice but candidates do not consider it rude for interviewers to take notes. The notes should, however, be only brief memory joggers and should not be an attempt to evaluate the candidate during the course of the interview.

Close

Interviewers need to bring interviews to a firm and decisive close, after consulting their check-list to make sure that there are no major gaps in the information that has been provided. Candidates should be invited to offer any other information that has not been covered in the main part of the interview and that he or she thinks important. The candidate should receive clear guidance on what is to happen next and when he or she should be expected to hear from the organisation.

Review

Judging the candidate should not take place until the interview has been completed. As soon as the interview has finished the interviewer should take time to conduct an evaluation rather than stepping straight into the next interview. A scoring system, particularly one linked to competencies, will help significantly. It is important to avoid making an assessment of the candidate during the course of the interview.

Pitfalls

Research into the effectiveness of interviews has revealed a number of pitfalls which are all too common.

Snap judgements

Judgements can be formed about the candidate far too quickly – within the first few seconds of meeting them – and the interview process then becomes the means by which evidence is gathered to reinforce that judgement. Some research has shown that many decisions on candidates are snap judgements made in the first two minutes of the interview.

Concentration

The concentration span of many interviewers follows a distinct pattern of a sharp downward dip in the main part of the interview with peaks of concentration in the first five minutes and the last five minutes of the interview. This is one of the reasons for note taking during the interview, not only to refresh the memory at a later stage but also as a prompt to continued concentration.

Ignoring the context

Interviewers can often discount the environment in which the candidate is working, when forming judgements. It is easy to attribute dynamism to a candidate performing well in a high-achievement organisation or culture when they may be swept away in the tide of performance rather than necessarily contributing to it directly. Equally, candidates working in a risk-averse culture may not be assessed as entrepreneurial or innovative in comparison with other candidates. It is important to seek information on the environment in which they are working and to judge answers in context.

Stereotyping

There is a danger in stereotyping both good and bad groups. This can be a particular problem for discriminating against ethnic minorities. Every candidate deserves to be regarded as unique and individual, and assessed as such.

Mirroring

There is a great danger of subjectivity creeping into the assessment of an interview so that people are rated positively or negatively according to whether they are similar or dissimilar to the interviewer. This is often a subconscious process and poses a particular risk in an unstructured interview. There have been many unfortunate examples of people in roles who bear an uncannily similar outlook to the interviewer but who occupy roles which the interviewer would not choose to fill. There are, of course, more obvious cases of where the candidate bears an uncanny similarity to the interviewer and has an identical surname . . .

12

ASSESSMENT CENTRES

The assessment centre is a process that involves a number of techniques and a number of assessors, breaking down the assessment of candidates into a number of components and then re-assembling them for a complete picture on which a decision is based. There are two main purposes for development centres:

- development
- selection.

The distinction between the two is sometimes blurred but, in essence, the development type will aim to assess the strengths and weaknesses of the candidate and provide a framework for utilising the strengths and addressing the weaknesses through developmental programmes and training. The focus of the development centre is often on the provision of information to the 'candidate' with great emphasis on feedback.

The selection-based assessment centre may be used for external selection or internal promotion or both. Its focus is on identifying the suitability of the candidate for a current or future planned position.

The distinction between the two types of assessment centre is not always so clear cut. Sometimes the purpose of the centre is to fill current or future positions, but considerable time is taken to provide feedback and development guidance to candidates. Sometimes development centres influence 'separate' decisions on selection for certain positions. The focus of this chapter is on the use of assessment centres for making selection decisions.

The origin of the assessment centre can be traced to World War II when it was used by the War Office Selection Board to select officers. World War I had cruelly exposed the incompetence of some officers and, in so doing, condemned a history of selection that owed more to social status than to leadership. The move, in the early part of the century, from commissions being bought to people being selected had begun a focus on capability but the process was compromised by the reliance on the judgement of selectors who suffered the prejudices of old. The War Office Selection Board devised a system of selection techniques which included exercises, tests and interviews. The system also placed the selection decision in the hands of a number of assessors, including a psychiatrist. The new system led to a significant improvement in the success rate of selection and was subsequently adopted by the USA for the selection of its intelligence staff.

Based on its wartime success, the assessment centre was adopted in different forms in the Civil Service and the public sector. In the USA some private sector organisations saw the potential of the development centre for use in identifying management potential, and AT & T and Standard Oil were at the forefront of its use. The 1980s saw a significant growth in the use of assessment centres both in the UK and the USA, with emphasis on their use for management selection and graduate recruitment.

It is difficult to define an assessment centre; its nature and content may differ significantly from one organisation to another. It is probably fair to say, however, that the key aspects are that:

- the assessment centre uses multiple selection techniques with each technique being only one piece of the jigsaw building up to the complete picture of the candidate
- the assessment centre uses a group of assessors, with selection decisions usually being made on a group basis.

A 'typical' assessment centre is likely to involve one or more interviews (sometimes one-to-one and sometimes panel interviews), a set of exercises, and ability or personality testing (or both). The assessment centre will involve a number of assessors who are usually trained in the specific assessment centre methodology being applied, and the assessors will usually be a mix of HR staff and line managers. The assessors will undertake active roles within the assessment centre process, usually interviewing and observing during exercises. In some assessment centres the assessors are assigned specific candidates whom they follow throughout the process, and then rate them. In others the assessor may be assigned to a part of the process and rate candidates only for that particular part. In both cases it is customary for all assessors to be involved in the final decision on candidates, which usually takes the form of a selection conference.

Design

Assessment centres are usually bespoke systems. It is very rare that an assessment centre is imported from one organisation to another or made available on a proprietary basis. The stages of the design are:

Stage 1   is to identify the key criteria upon which the assessment will be based. In practice this usually means that assessment centres are competency-based and, where a competency framework does not already exist, work will be undertaken through job analysis to identify the success criteria. This is covered in Chapter 6 on role analysis.

Stage 2   will be the choice of techniques to incorporate in the assessment centre, identifying the most suitable technique for each competency. Cost and time constraints may, of course, influence these decisions.

Stage 3   is the development of the techniques which may involve 'buying-in' or developing 'in-house'. For the interview this will mean the preparation of interview questions of either the situational type, based on the projected work for which the candidate is being assessed, or a behavioural type to identify the experiences of the candidate. It is, of course, possible for the assessment centre to use unstructured interviews but a well-designed assessment centre will inevitably use a well-designed and structured interview technique. For the test, whether buying-in or designing in-house, it will mean arranging the availability of suitably trained test administrators and ensuring test conditions. For the exercises, it will be a case of buying-in or developing and testing any bespoke exercises. Although there is a ready availability of interview material, psychological tests, and assessment exercises, it is usual to find that most assessment centres buy-in only psychological tests, and design their own interview structure and exercises.

Stage 4   The final stage is involved in the selection and training of assessors. In so doing consideration is given not only to the resourcing of the assessment centre (in having sufficient assessors available to support the process) but also to the involvement of line managers in the selection process. This adds realism to the assessment process as well as commitment and support to those chosen by means of it. Since the selection decisions will usually be group decisions involving all the assessors it is important that they are fully trained in the use of the assessment centre and in reaching conclusions from it. This invariably means the development of a rating system within the design of the exercises. It may, however, entail training in specific techniques, perhaps in test administration, or in interviewing skills, or in the process and skills of observation.

The design of an assessment centre is rarely a one-person job and is usually undertaken as a project which involves a steering group, of which the client will be a member, and which will determine policy aspects such as the budget for the assessment centre and the nomination of assessors. The size of the project team undertaking the design will depend upon the degree of original design needed, particularly whether or not success criteria, such as competencies, already exist in the organisation and whether an emphasis is to be placed on a buying-in or developing in-house. It is frequently the case that external consultants are used to advise and assist in the design process.

Components

The components of the assessment centre will include the interview, testing and exercises. Interviewing is covered in Chapter 11 and testing is covered in Chapter 10. The range of exercises can have their basis in:

- work simulations *or*
- competencies

and are characterised as either:

- group exercises *or*
- individual exercises.

It is usual to find more than one exercise involved in an assessment centre.

Work simulation exercises are designed to provide a realistic flavour of the scope and nature of the work which the candidate will be undertaking. On an individual basis this could mean an in-tray exercise in which a range of documents is given over a timed period to the individual, who is expected to clear the work and in so doing some of his or her competencies can be assessed. The object is not necessarily to clear the tray at all costs, so that the propensity to delegate may be only one factor under consideration; each of the pieces of paper would be designed to elicit information on certain competencies. There may, for example, be a letter of complaint aimed at identifying service orientation or empathy or diplomacy. There may be another piece of paper as an internal request for additional budgets or resources aimed at measuring decision-making. Thus the in-tray will comprise a number of mini-assessments. Carefully designed, it will replicate many of the occurrences in the work for which the candidate is being selected. An individual work simulation could also be a role play in which the assessor or an actor plays the role of a customer or a disgruntled foreman or a demanding boss etc and the candidate is given a briefing which includes objectives to be achieved from their meeting. This is a particularly useful technique for assessing interpersonal skills. The individual exercises do not, however, have to be work simulations; they can be abstract so that a written exercise may be given to the candidate to gauge, for example, problem-solving which contains puzzles of a non-work kind, or they may be asked to write a summary of the day's news in order to assess their report-writing abilities and analytical skills. The advantage of individual exercises is that they can in certain circumstances be more administratively convenient and they help to filter out 'disturbance' from competing candidates which could interfere with individual assessment as part of a group exercise. The abstract exercises provide a level playing field in that they do not demand prior knowledge or experience, but they can appear as school tests rather than serious selection. The simulations may favour candidates with the relevant experience but they have the advantage of giving the candidates a feel for the nature of the work in which they will be involved.

Work simulations can be directed at a group basis and include role plays in which the group is given a work-related project to consider and plan. This may be designed to assess leadership qualities or team-working or problem-solving or some other competency. There are other exercises in which the assessed group is subsumed within a larger group. Thus, for example, the group may be subjected to 'trial by sausage roll' in which they are invited to an 'informal' buffet to meet with current employees to find out more about the work. In so doing they are observed by assessors who will gauge their skill in identifying key influencers, instigating discussions, handling dialogue, and 'working the room'. This is a particularly effective technique for selecting political candidates but it also has much to commend it for 'social' roles such as sales representatives or project managers where the role will involve dealing with people in a variety of settings and maintaining control and purpose in establishing dialogue. It is good practice to advise the candidates that the 'informal' gathering is an exercise to be formally assessed.

Some assessment centres use group exercises in an abstract setting asking teams, for example, to play out desert survival games or build log bridges or lego castles. They may be asked to enter into general discussions or to make a presentation to the rest of the group with the observers assessing either the presentation skills of the presenter or the team skills of the 'audience'.

Regardless of whether the exercises are set at group or individual level, or whether they are work simulations or abstract, the purpose of the exercise should be clearly defined and the competencies to be measured by it should be kept firmly in view. In general terms, the more abstract the exercise the more uncomfortable the participants tend to be with it. Thus the abstract exercises tend to be found more frequently where the target group is school leavers or graduates. The cost and resource availability will dictate the scale of the exercises, of course. Some organisations are able to use sophisticated exercises such as flight simulators for pilots or simulated call centres for tele-sales staff and these can provide very effective and realistic assessments. Where abstract exercises are being used care must be taken to ensure that the competencies that they ought to measure are relevant to the work; one high street bank used to conduct three-week assessment centres at their staff college, and the assessment included observation of their dining skills, including correct use of the cutlery and the direction in which they passed the port. Whatever exercises are designed, it is essential to pilot and test them to check that the timings are appropriate, that the instructions are clear and unambiguous, and that they achieve the balance of giving enough direction to ensure the candidates undertake them, but without prompting them in any direction. In designing the exercises, the rating form is also designed so that the assessors are clear on the particular competencies that they are attempting to rate.

Advantages and disadvantages

There are many advantages to using assessment centres.

- They focus on the key elements of the role and are therefore very specific in measuring the suitability of candidates.
- They are thorough, avoiding over-reliance on a single technique but ensuring that a range of techniques is used to

gather a full picture and a range of assessors employed to obtain a balanced picture. By using a variety of techniques the overall validity of the process is enhanced.

- Assessment centres can be interesting for the candidates since they provide a variety of activities and often the opportunity to meet with other candidates and, through the involvement of assessors, a greater number of people from the organisation than is usually available with other techniques.

- The assessment exercises in particular can provide a useful flavour of the work, which can be important in ensuring that the candidate is making the right choice.

- Some studies have shown that assessment centres are more effective than other techniques at predicting successful candidates (but care needs to be taken with this conclusion since assessment centres are most frequently used for the selection of high flyers and there is therefore an element of self-fulfilling prophecy in operation).

Assessment centres also have some disadvantages.

- The process can feel uncomfortable to some candidates, particularly at a senior level, and particularly where abstract exercises are involved. Candidates can be offended by being asked to build lego blocks when decisions about their career are on the line.

- Assessment centres are sometimes transparent and it is all too easy for candidates to 'act' in group exercises and other aspects, which may be sustained for the few days or weeks of the assessment centre, but not fulfilled in the real world.

- The centres can be time-consuming for the organisation and for the candidates. While school-leavers and graduates may be able to devote time to assessment centres, those currently in employment will have difficulty devoting more than half a day. Where exercises are involved, the high ratio of observers to candidates makes it time-consuming and therefore costly for the organisation. Added to the active involvement there is also the time needed to be trained (and up-dated) and take part in the decision-making.

- One of the prerequisites of assessment centre exercises is that they should be appropriate to the general level of intellect and experience of the candidates. This therefore means that some stereotyping has already taken place and the danger of discrimination is present, but not easily recognised. More easily recognised is the discrimination implicit in exercises that involve physical activities.

PART 4

DECISIONS

13

DECISION-MAKING

Decisions

The key purpose of selection activity is, of course, to match the candidate(s) to the position(s) and, however complex or simple, however long or short, ultimately a decision needs to be made. Even where there is only one candidate, a decision still needs to be made on whether or not to offer the position to that candidate (and such 'Hobson's Choice' can often be the most difficult). In some cases it may be possible to defer the decision by offering the candidate a temporary position or work trial to provide more time and evidence. In most cases, however, a decision needs to be taken on the evidence available and however good the technique, it usually requires an element of judgement.

The two key elements in making the final selection are:

- gathering the evidence
- making the decision.

This may seem obvious, but selection is not unlike other aspects of managerial decision-making where the practice sometimes becomes 'ready, fire, aim' and evidence is gathered to justify decisions rather than shape them.

Gathering the evidence

The development of the specification at the beginning of the selection process should form the framework for making the decision, and therefore the checklist, for ensuring that all data have been gathered.

In using a non-competency based approach the PERSON-specification will be checked to ensure that there is evidence of the **P**ersonal qualities, the **E**xperience required, the **R**ecord of achievement desired, the **S**kills and qualifications needed, the fit with the **O**rganisation, and whether the **N**eeds of the candidate are likely to be fulfilled in this position.

Using the competency-based approach the process is slightly easier because there is a logical structure. Each of the competencies being sought is clear, and the framework for the choice of selection tools will provide a map of where the evidence can be found. Figure 6 shows how a specification can be compared directly with an 'audit trail' showing where evidence of each competency has been found.

Both the PERSON method and the competency-based method follow the 'whole picture' approach rather than the 'hurdle' approach.

Figure 6

USING DIFFERENT TECHNIQUES TO SEARCH FOR EVIDENCE OF REQUIRED COMPETENCIES

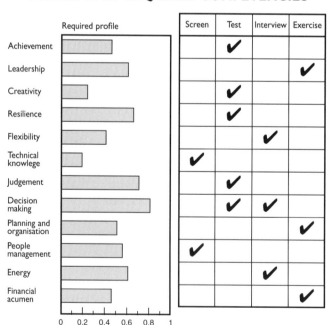

Required profile	Screen	Test	Interview	Exercise
Achievement		✔		
Leadership				✔
Creativity		✔		
Resilience		✔		
Flexibility			✔	
Technical knowlege	✔			
Judgement		✔		
Decision making		✔	✔	
Planning and organisation				✔
People management	✔			
Energy			✔	
Financial acumen				✔

0   0.2   0.4   0.6   0.8   1

In the 'hurdle' approach, each part of the selection process is regarded as an entity in its own right. Thus, for example, the application screen, once completed, will progress short-listed candidates to the next stage, but the information gathered in making the short-listing decision will be jettisoned. The next stage may perhaps be a test and initial interview which will allow some candidates to come forward to a final interview which will then be the sole decision point. The final interview will determine whether the candidate is offered the position; all earlier stages will have been steps along the way or 'hurdles' that the candidate will successfully negotiate in order to be eligible for the final selection.

In the 'whole picture' approach, there may still be a 'whittling-down' activity in the same way as the 'hurdle' approach, with fewer candidates at the final stage than at the first screening. The difference, however, is that the information from all parts of the selection process is assembled and the decision formed on the basis of all of it. Thus the 'whole picture' would include the assessment and rating of the application form, the results of the test and the outcome of all the interviews; a balanced view is then taken based on the complete range of information.

The terms adopted by psychologists for the two approaches are non-compensatory (hurdle) and compensatory (whole picture). Research into the two approaches shows that the 'whole picture' approach provides significantly greater success in making selection decisions than using the 'hurdle' approach. It is particularly useful when used with a competency-based selection structure because the components do not overlap or duplicate each other, thereby avoiding potential conflict and unnecessary cost.

It is a useful discipline to use an evidence organiser for candidate information throughout the selection process. The organiser maintains records for scores or assessments at each stage of the process so that a single form can be used instead of trying to collect the information from different documents. The use of computer software packages to support the selection process can help significantly in presenting information, for example providing an analysis across candidates at each stage, or across all stages for each candidate.

Consideration will need to be given to whether the information from each of the selection stages will be assessed on a common scale. For example, should the application screen be subdivided into five scales of acceptability, the interview rating in a similar format and the test sten scores clustered into five standard scores? This aspect will be most significant if the actuarial approach to decision-making, discussed below, is used.

Making the decision

There are two main approaches to selection decisions:

- actuarial
- interpretative.

The actuarial approach is very mechanistic and objective. The scores for each stage of the selection process are added together and the position(s) offered to the candidate(s) with the highest score(s). It may be the case that certain stages are weighted to give greater emphasis. For example, using a non-weighted approach, candidates A and B may be assessed on a five point scale as follows:

	A	B
Application	3	3
Test	4	3
First interview	4	5
Exercise	4	4
Second interview	4	5
Total scores	**19**	**20**

and candidate B would be offered the job. A similar approach can be used where each competency is assessed and scored, again using a five point scale for illustration:

	A	B
Planning and organising	3	4
Relationships	4	5
Knowledge	3	3
Judgement	4	3
Adaptability	4	5
Total scores	**18**	**20**

In the second example, each of the competencies would be assessed from different stages or techniques but with some perhaps being measured by more than one technique (assuming, for example, that judgement is measured by a test plus an interview then the final score would be the average of the two).

Both of these examples assume that equal importance would be attached to each stage (in the first example) or each competency (in the second example). It may, of course, be the case that greater importance is to be attached to one or another, and a weighting system would be applied. Using the same examples, if the test in the first example received a weighting of 2.0 and the exercise received a weighting of 1.5, then both candidates would have equal scores. In the second example, weighting competencies of 'relationships' and 'adaptability' by 1.5 would increase the advantage of B over A.

There are some considerations with the actuarial approach. First, weightings need to be determined at the start of the process rather than 'modelled' at the end to fit the desired outcome. Second, the greater the scale the more meaningful the differences and the usefulness of final scores, and a ten-point scale is particularly useful. Third, when weighting is attached to stages it can either be used to underline the importance of that stage or to 'balance' it if there are concerns (about the validity or consistency or whatever) about that stage.

The advantage of the actuarial approach is that it is transparent and consistent. It is easy to see 'fairness' of the outcome, and even with weightings it ensures a balanced reliance on all elements of the selection process. The disadvantages are first that it can 'dilute' significant failings at any one stage – for example a poor 'fit' between the organisation and candidate – which although only part of the process may be a fundamental flaw. Second, it tends not to work too well in practice in that it feels overly mechanistic, and successful candidates may be those of a 'middle-ground' character rather than the noticeable candidates. For this reason it can be unpopular with selectors.

The interpretative approach is similar in some ways to the actuarial in that all stages are considered and, usually, scored. The difference, however, is that the decision is not automatic;

the evidence is analysed and a judgement made. In so doing, the selector may decide, for example, to downplay a lack of experience gleaned from the application form, because of a good grasp of the issues displayed in the interview. More importantly, perhaps, the interpretative approach, when used for competency-based selection, allows for finer judgement so that, for example, while marginal scores in relationships and adaptability may not in themselves detract from overall scores, their combined significance may cause the selector to reject the candidate. In this way, the interpretative approach allows for the interplay of competencies to be considered and therefore to provide a more refined decision.

It is frequently the case in the interpretative approach that a graphical representation of scores, such as a bar chart, is used instead of plain scores since it helps decision-makers in gaining a clearer overview of the candidate. An example of this appears in Figure 7.

Figure 7
USING BAR CHARTS TO COMPARE CANDIDATES WITH THE JOB SPECIFICATION

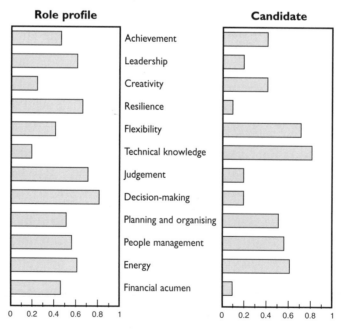

Mistakes

Selection is not a perfect science. Mistakes occur, and from time to time there are serious errors of judgement. Sometimes such errors simply lead to the most suitable candidate not being selected, sometimes it leads to a poor candidate being selected, and sometimes it leads to discrimination against candidates. There are some common errors in decision-making which need to be guarded against.

- Ignoring the specification may seem an obvious mistake but one that is not always so easily avoided since there can be a danger of the selection assignment becoming a competition rather than a search, and candidates are compared with each other rather than compared with the specification. In the same way that an auction bidder sets bid limits and negotiators predetermine remits, so too must selectors ensure that the parameters they set, through the specification, are adhered to in the final decision-making. Where no candidates match the specification, and there is no opportunity to redesign the role to accommodate shortfalls, appointments should not be made.

- Over-reliance on a single element can sometimes lead to mistakes where, for example, a first class interview performance is allowed to eclipse concerns about past experience or test results. There may, of course, be occasions where a reasoned decision is made to 'allow' for some shortcomings but, in general, the purpose of a multiple-technique approach to selection is to gain a balanced picture, and over-reliance on any single element will give a distorted view.

- The halo effect is a variation on this theme and it occurs where a particular virtue of the candidate is allowed to obscure or downplay negative factors. It is particularly prevalent in interviewing, where a candidate may give an answer which provides positive indicators of competencies but is not then probed for any negative examples, to see both sides of the coin. In the overall decision-making, the halo effect can sometimes occur because, for example, the university attended or a specific company experience can carry weight with the decision-maker and the negative aspects of the candidate's assessment are downplayed or ignored.

- Stereotyping occurs positively and negatively. In positive stereotyping, people of a certain age or background or experience in common with others employed, but of no causal relationship to performance, are deemed to be suitable candidates. In negative stereotyping a similar process occurs to the detriment of the candidate. It is inevitable in selection that selectors will drift to categories of people, but lumping people together because of their physical attributes, social background or skin colour is a generalisation that is so wildly inaccurate that it turns selection into a lottery. A carefully-drafted specification should help to ensure that proper selection penetrates such superficial categorisation.

- Mirroring or 'similarity-identity bias' occurs where the selector favours a candidate, usually subconsciously, because the candidate matches the selector's own outlook, experience, etc. It is a particularly prevalent mistake in interviewing where the interviewer 'gets on well' with the candidate and establishes rapport because of a common interest etc. This is a very common problem where a specification has not been properly drafted or agreed with the client, and it is not uncommon for some personnel staff to select candidates 'in their own image' for positions for which they (the personnel staff) would be neither suitable or motivated.

- Prejudice occurs both consciously and unconsciously. There are, sadly, still incidents of people being rejected because of physical disabilities or age or social background or ethnicity. The moral (and legal) perspective is condemnatory but equally lamentable is the harsh truth that organisations are denied suitable (and sometimes the most suitable) candidates because of the personal failings of selectors. Prejudice is not always oppositional; in one recent study, female interviewees suffered gender bias in interviews but the bias did not come from male interviewers (who displayed no bias to either gender in the interview and subsequent decision-making) but from female interviewers who identified themselves with successful males and were gender-biased against female candidates.

- Non-involvement of clients in the selection process and in decision-making may adversely affect the successful integration of the new appointee and therefore corrupt the decision retroactively. It would be rare indeed for an external selection consultant not to involve his or her client in an interview and to go further than making a recommendation for the client's final decision. In the case of internal selectors, it may still be the case from time to time that decisions are made on behalf of internal clients, or the client is bullied or blinded into decisions. The interpersonal rapport between a new appointee and his or her new manager is important to success and such 'chemistry' should not be ignored. Equally, the involvement of line managers (and future colleagues) in the selection decision will make them more committed to the success of the new person.

14

CHECKS AND OFFERS

Checking

While it is the case that more than half UK employers surveyed on recruitment practices (Industrial Relations Services survey, 1996) declared that they take up references before a job offer is made, it is very rarely the case that references and other checks are undertaken before a decision is made on the candidate. This chapter is therefore concerned with the steps that need to be undertaken to verify claims by the candidate being offered a position, whether or not the offer is made before, after, or subject to, the checks. There are three main areas for checking:

- document checks
- statutory checks
- references.

Documents

Document checking is concerned with verifying that the qualifications, certificates etc, claimed by the candidate can be substantiated. Documents may include personal certificates such as birth and marriage certificates, which may be relevant to the job in terms of minimum age but are more frequently a requirement for satisfying pension scheme eligibility. Since qualifications ought only to be sought and mentioned where they are pertinent to job performance, it follows that any claims ought to be verified and the original documents checked. This should be an obvious point, and a simple practice, but the author's own experience and anecdotal evidence of others suggests that it is a frequent flaw in recruitment practices; the incidence of bogus professionals operating in even the most regulated professions may be more commonplace than generally thought. Any licences claimed by the applicant, and pertinent to the role, should also be checked – particularly driving licences, HGV licences, fork-lift truck licences, pilot's licence etc, not least because the employer will be vicariously liable for any accidents arising in the course of employment. Where membership of professional associations is claimed, they should also be checked; most provide a certificate of membership and some publish a register or yearbook (but exercise care with omissions which may be a printer's error or lapsed subscriptions rather than non-membership). It is a question of convenience whether these checks are undertaken during the course of the selection process, such as at the interview, or whether the checks are undertaken before employment is started or on the day it is started. It is, however, good practice to advise all applicants that any qualifications/licences (etc) claimed will be checked. It is prudent to keep a record of the check and/or a photocopy of the certificates on the employee's file, in the event of any future legal action being taken by a third party against the employer as being vicariously liable for the employee.

Statutory

There are certain statutory obligations which must be fulfilled by an employer. Employees must be registered for National Insurance contributions and it is the duty of an employer to ensure that there is such registration for National Insurance purposes. At one time, employees were provided with National Insurance cards which an employer could obtain but nowadays the only 'proof' is a National Insurance number which the employee should quote when taking up work. There is still some leeway for employers to allow the employment to begin, and to make payments to the employee, but this can only be a short-term arrangement and if the employee cannot provide a National Insurance number within 14 days of beginning employment, the employment must be suspended until such time as a number can be obtained. The Department of Social Security will help in the provision of temporary National Insurance numbers where there are particular difficulties.

The Asylum and Immigration Act 1996 makes it a criminal offence to employ any person over 16 who is subject to immigration control unless that person has current and valid permission to be in the UK (ie a work permit) and that permission does not prevent him or her from taking the job in question, or the person comes into a category where the employment is otherwise allowed (for example *au pair*). There is no small measure of difficulty with this requirement. It is an offence of strict liability which means that it is irrelevant whether the employer knew the law, or whether the employer was unaware, or did not suspect, that the employee needed such a document. Citizens of member states of the European Community are entitled to move freely within it and are not required to provide any form of certificate. Similarly, Commonwealth citizens may be exempt from immigration controls. It is an offence to deny someone employment because of their nationality (under the Race Relations Act 1976) and there may be a presumption of racial discrimination if a non-white is asked questions about work permits or immigration restrictions at interview (unless all applicants are asked the question). The different aims of different pieces of separately drafted legislation can therefore 'cause a headache' for the employer trying to work within them. The employer can mount a defence to prosecution under the Asylum and Immigration Act by showing that eligibility for employment was correctly checked through National Insurance number, passport, work permit etc, (if there is a copy for proof) and it would seem prudent therefore to ensure that 'start to work' information is properly secured and separated from the application form or other selection documents. The Act applies only where there is a direct employment relationship.

References

References seem to be an almost universal requirement and nearly all employers seek them. Some employers will not provide references, some will not provide references where an offer has already been made 'subject to' satisfactory ones being received. Even where employers operate such policies, they are not embarrassed about seeking references for their candidates. References may take a number of forms:

- references from schools or universities, often focusing on academic achievement. Some head teachers decline to provide references because of the sheer workload and the availability of Records of Achievement which should provide the evidence employers require.

- personal or character references which generally show that the new employee is a decent sort of person (whatever that may be) and may be sought from friends, colleagues, acquaintances or, more frequently, 'reputable' people in professional positions. The local JP, GP, and vicar have not been spared such burdens by the advance in selection methods.

- work references may be the most sought-after. Sometimes such references are simply an open request for information about the candidate, sometimes they may be a closed questionnaire seeking specific information to verify claims made etc, perhaps asking specific questions on employment dates, attendance record, work performance, relationships with people, and other pertinent information from their past. Sometimes the reference seeks the views of the current or former employer on the suitability of the candidate to undertake the post for which he or she has applied, in which case it is important to provide information about the role and the qualities and competencies needed to perform it.

- specialist references such as credit history, medical history and criminal record. Credit checks are more frequently undertaken for positions where cash-handling or other financial transactions are important, and are therefore commonplace in financial institutions which are characterised by such work, and where access to the information is more readily available. Medical history may be sought in over-zealous concern for attendance or because it has a significant bearing on the employment (eg flying or sea-diving) and may be accompanied by a requirement to undergo a medical examination. There is a requirement for the individual to consent to the release of such information. Access to criminal history will become easier as a consequence of the Police Act 1997 which created the Criminal Records Agency which, from 1998, provides Criminal Record Certificates to employers in occupations that are exceptions under the Rehabilitation of Offenders Act, together with enhanced criminal record certificates (for those working on a regular unsupervised basis with children) giving information on convictions and non-conviction information. Fees are payable for the certificates.

There are variations in the timing of references. Some employers choose to take up references for candidates at one of the stages in the selection process, usually the interview. Some take up references when they have decided to select the candidate, but before an offer is made. Some seek references after the offer is made, sometimes making such an offer 'subject to receipt of satisfactory references'. Some will be happy to receive references after the employee has started. Seeking references during the selection process should be undertaken only where they are needed to contribute to the selection decision, otherwise it is administratively inefficient, wasting time also for the referees. Where references are taken up in this way, it is essential that candidates are advised beforehand that it is the practice and their consent is obtained. It is particularly important that, whatever the stage at which they are sought, references from current employers are not sought without the clear knowledge of the candidate, for it would not be unusual for such requests to put the employee's current or future job prospects at risk. Some referees take offence at being asked to provide a reference for someone who has been offered a job 'subject to receipt of satisfactory references', and some companies adopt a policy of refusing to provide references in such circumstances. Particular issues apply in relation to internal references which, as Table 16 explains, can often form an important element of the selection process.

There is great unease about references, both in the giving and the taking. Referees must ensure that they provide

Table 16
USING REFERENCES FOR WORKPLACE ASSESSMENT

References are often regarded as a form of check or safeguard rather than being part of the selection process. It is possible to use references as a form of workplace assessment. Good results have been achieved through the use of 360-degree appraisal, in which managers, colleagues and subordinates assess the performance of an individual and their likelihood of succeeding in a new role. It is, however, a complicated process to establish purely for selection decisions. If organisations are already using 360-degree appraisal it will be worthwhile considering its use for selection purposes.

Some organisations, such as the Coastguard Agency, seek references from an applicant's manager when there is an internal application.

Along with space for general comments and candidates' 'particular qualities' and areas for improvement, their Internal Reference Form specifically asks 'referee' managers to 'comment in detail on the following attributes, based on current performance and potential:

- knowledge of the Coastguard Association
- operational command qualities
- interpersonal skills
- resource management (financial, time, materials, etc)
- administration, drafting and representational skills.'

Such methods have proved very successful in generating realistic reports.

truthful, accurate and reliable information, and hold a legal liability, to take care, to those to whom they supply a reference (*Hedley Byrne* v *Heller, 1964*) and to those who are the subject of the reference (*Spring* v *Guardian Assurance, 1994*). Failure to disclose relevant information will create as much liability as providing false information. There is a view that employers are under a legal obligation to their employees to provide references on their behalf where future work is dependent upon them; as yet this has not been established in any cases. Given that referees are rarely paid for the service they provide it is interesting to see why they provide it; it is perhaps because they are concerned that if everyone 'drops out of the game' they will be denied access to information in times when they need it. It is all the more curious, therefore, to note that many employers are cynical about the value of the information they receive in references. This is particularly the case in 'open' references where reading between the lines is often more important than reading what is on them. Thus, statements such as 'he left us fired with enthusiasm' or 'you will be lucky to get her to work for you' may be capable of more than one meaning. Expressions such as 'attentive to detail' (nit-picking), 'co-operative' (follows the herd), 'independent' (stubborn), 'supportive' (sucks up to the boss) and 'flexible' (indecisive) sometimes need careful decoding. There has been little research into the effectiveness of references but those few studies that have been undertaken in the UK have indicated a positive correlation in that 'good reference' predicted 'good performer'. Most employers, however, approach references as a safety net, as a means of checking that the information given to them by the candidate is factual. To this end, references can be more reliable when they are sought as a questionnaire that elicits specific answers to specific questions which may include:

- the period of employment
- work performance, usually providing a simple scale from *poor* through *acceptable*, *good* and *very good* to *excellent*
- time lost due to sickness or other absence
- reason for leaving (if already left)
- a question on whether the employer would re-employ
- a catch-all question seeking any other relevant information and/or reasons why he or she should not be employed.

Referees generally find it easier to complete pre-formatted questionnaires and the information tends to be more reliable and more speedily returned. An example appears in Table 17. It is not always the case that references are written; often they are sought by telephone and, even when a written reference is obtained, a follow-up phone call may be used or offered. It is often felt that a more accurate picture will be obtained over the telephone than in writing, but note that liability for false or misleading information applies as much to oral representations as to written information!

Reference agencies
A more recent trend in the USA, and likely to catch on in the UK, has been the use of reference-checking agencies.

Table 17

EXAMPLE OF A LETTER SEEKING REFERENCE

REQUEST FOR REFERENCE

Mr/Ms ....

has applied for the post of ....

and has advised that you are prepared to provide a reference on his/her behalf.

How long have you known him/her? ....

In what capacity? ....

Please assess the following:

	Poor	Acceptable	Good	Excellent
Attitude to work				
Abilities				
Productivity				
Working with people				
Honesty				
Attendance				

Do you know any reason why we should not employ? ....

If employed by you, please state   date joined ....

date left ....

would you re-employ? ....

Signature .... Date ....

Please return in the envelope provided or telephone ....

For a fixed fee the agency will undertake to obtain references from former employers, and check out any specific aspects such as credit, health, and criminal history. The benefit of using such an agency is that by specialising they develop expertise in procuring the information, they know how to conform with all the appropriate legal and ethical standards, and by focusing on the task they can devote time to chasing the information and thereby free selectors from the chore.

Offers

Conditions

Offers of employment may be conditional or unconditional. An unconditional offer is one where the post is offered to the candidate without any 'strings' attached, and it is left to the candidate to determine whether or not to accept. Conditional offers fall into two main types of:

- pre-conditions
- post-conditions.

Typical pre-conditions include making the offer 'subject to receipt of satisfactory references' or subject to attainment of certain qualifications or educational grades. Such pre-conditions should clearly be treated by both the employer and potential employee as deferring the appointment to the new role until such time as the conditions have been met. They should also signal that failure to achieve the conditions will mean that the offer is withdrawn. Post-conditional offers may include an appointment 'subject to completion of a satisfactory probationary period' or (less common nowadays) taking up residence within a certain time period. It should be clear that where such conditions are not subsequently met, the employment will terminate. In practice such clarity does not always follow, and while pre-conditions are often regarded by both parties as essential prerequisites, post-conditions somehow come to be regarded, by either or both parties, as a mere formality. Even where formal processes exist for the review of probationary periods, termination seems to occur less frequently than 'duff' appointments.

Whatever conditions are attached to the appointment, they must be clearly communicated and acknowledged. Similarly, the terms of any offer should be clear and unequivocal. There may be positions where the appointment is subject to some flexibility on pay and some negotiation may take place between the employer and the candidate. Where such negotiation is likely to take place, employers will find themselves in a stronger position if they discuss pay during the selection process (for example at interview) rather than at the point of offer, when the candidate will know that he or she is in a stronger negotiating position (because they are the preferred or only suitable candidate and refusal will subject the employer to further costs of re-advertising etc). Negotiations ought, however, to take place in good faith and any indications of employment conditions during the recruitment assignment should be realistic; advertisements, for example, should carry a figure approximate to the amount the new candidate will earn rather than some hypothetical long-term salary. It is, of course, quite in order to put forward long-term earnings or on-target earnings but, in so doing, the figures should be clearly described as such. This is not simply good manners but prudently avoids the disappointment of candidates rejecting offers, or new employees leaving prematurely. In constructing the offer, it should be borne in mind that many candidates falsely inflate their current earnings in an attempt to improve their future prospects.

Legal considerations

It needs to be remembered that employment is a legal contract. While the new hire may not become an employee until the employment begins, the contract itself is legally enforceable as soon as it is formed. It is formed when:

- there is an offer, and acceptance of the offer
- both parties intend it to be a legally binding arrangement
- there is 'consideration' (something of value attached to the contract)
- there is sufficient certainty of terms.

With the exception of apprentices and merchant seamen, there is no requirement for an employment contract to be in writing for it to be legally enforceable. An offer made and accepted at interview or over the phone etc, will therefore be legally enforceable, and provide the candidate with the right to claim for breach of contract if the accepted offer is withdrawn. It used to be thought that such an action would need to be pursued through the courts but the Employment Appeal Tribunal, in *Sarker* v *South Tees Acute Hospitals NHS Trust (1997)*, held that Industrial Tribunals are able to adjudicate on a breach of contract, prior to commencement of 'employment', in accordance with the Industrial Tribunals Extension of Jurisdiction Order 1994.

Although there is no requirement for the contract of employment to be in writing, there is a statutory requirement on employers to provide new employees with a written statement of the main terms and conditions of employment within two months of commencing work. Although the statement may be issued in instalments, and reference made to other documents such as handbooks or staff codes, certain terms must be in a single document known as 'the principal statement'. The principal statement will need to include:

- the name of the employer and employee
- the date employment began
- whether any previous period of employment counts as part of the employee's continuous employment
- any terms about holidays
- job title or job description and place of work or mobility clause
- the scale or rate of remuneration, the method of calculating, and the intervals at which it is paid
- hours of work, including any rules on overtime
- sick pay and pension arrangements (if any)
- the length of notice to be given on either side
- details of any collective bargaining agreements affecting the contract.

The last point is significant in illustrating that the terms of an employment contract may be express, implied, and incorporated. 'Incorporated terms' means those which are 'imported' from elsewhere. Thus, if the employee is employed on terms that are negotiated locally or centrally with the employer, or perhaps the employer's federation, then any changes which the trade union negotiates will 'automatically' form part of the employee's contract. 'Express terms' are those which are directly agreed between the employer and the employee but 'express' does not necessarily mean written; a term offered orally will bind the employer regardless of any subsequent attempt to substitute inferior terms in writing (unless the employee accepts). It is therefore important that any offers made at the interview, over the phone or any other low-key mode are clear, unambiguous and made with full authority, for they will form a binding contract (even if the person making the offer was not fully authorised to do so). 'Implied terms' come into play when there are no express or incorporated terms to cover them. They are 'read into' the contract and come about either through custom and practice or by common law or statute. Common law is the body of cases which set out legal precedent, such as the duty to provide work for the employee, the duty to provide mutual respect etc. The statutes provide a significant source of implied terms, particularly Health & Safety at Work legislation providing duties of care etc, and the various Discrimination Acts which provide that less favourable terms may not be offered to candidates on grounds of sex, race or disability. People covered by such legislation will be able either to accept the employment and then use the law to enforce terms which are not less favourable, or reject the offer and pursue a claim for discrimination.

In practice, most employers have an established set of terms and conditions of employment, and employment is clearly and explicitly offered within such terms. A leading New Zealand lawyer once noted 'the paradoxical truth is that a lengthy agreement in writing which sets out the terms relating to all conceivable contingencies produces a less complex contract than the one created by the word and the nod'.

PART 5

FOLLOW-UP

15

INDUCTION AND

DEVELOPMENT

Induction

Selection is not a noble art pursued for its own purpose, it is not an abstract exercise or quest for achievement in which the appointment of the most suitable candidate is the culmination of the challenge. It is a work process, a production line for securing and feeding human fodder into the organisation to provide sustenance to the organisation. Bizarre caricatures, perhaps, but useful to illustrate the point that selection does not end when the candidate takes up the role. There is a cost to selection, not only in the direct cost of finding and selecting people, but also the indirect cost of disruption and learning curves. Recruitment and selection must therefore be concerned with the length of time the new person will stay in the role, how quickly they can achieve full performance, and how well performance and commitment can be sustained.

The single most important influence on labour turnover is length of service. The simple truth is, that the longer an employee has been with an organisation the less likely they are to leave. Conversely those most at risk of leaving are new employees. The term 'induction crisis' has been coined to describe the first 12 months of an employee's service in which he or she will be most at risk of leaving. The first 12 weeks will be a particularly acute risk period, but normal stability does not really occur until after 12 months of service. Most organisations will find that, even if their labour turnover rates are in low single figures, labour turnover for the twelve month 'induction crisis' will be about 20 per cent. Good recruitment and selection practices must therefore be concerned with stabilising the risk and managing the integration of the new person into the role.

The first part of the induction begins long before the role is taken up. Information provided to the candidate throughout the selection process should be aimed at encouraging enthusiasm and managing expectations. In order to improve self-selection in the selection process, sufficient information should already have been given to the candidate to enable him or her to have a very clear idea of how the role will shape up.

Once an offer has been extended and accepted, work can begin on the induction process without waiting for the new employee physically to begin work. Some organisations begin the induction process as soon as an offer is made, not waiting until the candidate accepts, so that enthusiasm and commitment can be engendered in candidates who may be wavering in their decision. There is a danger of trying to load too much information on to people before they start, because there will inevitably be pressure on them in their old role to clear up and hand over. Where a relocation is involved, there will also be a great deal of domestic arrangements to be handled. Nevertheless, information on the organisation, its purpose, and 'culture' to supplement and expand on information already given, will help to create 'mental readiness'. There is not a great deal of point in loading organisation charts on to the new person, since these can be particularly bewildering, and only become meaningful when faces and personalities can be attached to the names, after starting. In technical or managerial positions, it is particularly useful to provide background information on current projects and initiatives and other issues as part of the mental preparation required for taking up the new challenges.

Planned induction

Once started, the new employee should follow a carefully planned induction programme which balances help and utilisation, so that plenty of assistance is provided to enable him or her to settle in and be able to do their work, but avoiding their attendance becoming just a 'learning' experience without getting a return on their time. The more clearly defined the role, and the greater the degree of homogeneity between organisations, then the easier it will be for the new person to adapt and become truly productive. A maintenance fitter, for example, may be able to make an immediate contribution on the first day while a supervisor or manager will need a great degree of familiarisation with people, processes, equipment etc, before being able to make a particularly meaningful contribution. A balance also needs to be struck between ensuring that there is sufficient information provided to speed up the induction process, while avoiding 'information overload' which will make it unnecessarily difficult for the new person to absorb all the information and is therefore counterproductive. It is useful, therefore, to plan the process over a few weeks rather than trying to cram everything into the first few days.

On the first day, new employees will need to be provided with 'signposts' to help them help themselves. This will include a guide to the workplace (including not only the 'physical' layout of the workplace, building or site but also the 'virtual layout' of computer systems and other tools). Health, safety and hygiene issues will need to be covered during the first day. Introduction should be kept to a minimum, and limited to those with whom the new hire will be in most contact, but taking care not to 'snub' anyone who feels they should have been introduced. 'Introduction' is more than social introduction, it is spending time with the people to get an understanding of their role and, more pertinently to begin building the relationship. Perhaps the most important outcome of the first day is that the new employee should go home with a good feeling for the organisation and its style, and the reassurance, through a warm welcome and a professional induction, that he or she has made the right decision.

By the end of the first week, new employees should have a clear understanding of the values and aims of the organisation, the aims and objectives of the immediate work group, a clear working knowledge of the purpose of their own role, and know their key (external and internal) contacts. The temptation to include any further 'general' induction topics during the first week should be avoided, and attention paid in the remainder of the time to the job itself. Thus, machine operators will need to be familiarised with the operation of their machine and all related aspects, sales or marketing people will need to be familiarised with products and related issues, delivery people will need to be familiarised with routes, cycles, customers, etc. The 'technical' aspects of the job will, in a well-run organisation, be set out in training schedules for the various positions, which are likely to form the training plan for a number of weeks or months. The 'general' issues which should be deferred beyond the first week are the aspects related to administration or bureaucracy which, although important (particularly for large organisations), are not urgent. Aspects such as the discipline or grievance procedures, claiming expenses, the performance appraisal scheme, and similar aspects need to be so considered. It is also important at this stage, however, to ensure that the new employee is provided with reference points or sources so that he or she can take responsibility for continuing their longer-term induction, and is not unduly hampered in making progress on work issues by not knowing who or where to ask.

In organisations where there is a fairly regular intake of new staff (at whatever level), it is very useful to plan a regular general induction day (or half-day). By setting a regular pattern, whether fortnightly, monthly or six weekly, it becomes easier for the organisation to slot new entrants on to the programme, whereas organising on an *ad hoc* basis is not only more work but also more uncertain in that there may not be 'enough time to get around to' organising the individual induction. It may, of course, seem unsuitable to have a general induction programme when the recruitment intake may be spread across a whole variety of posts and a spread of people across the 'pecking order' of the organisation. In practice, however, it works very well since people on the programme will have built up a relationship with others across the various parts of the organisation (even if the relationship is only a smiling nod in the staff restaurant) which can be important in reinforcing team culture. Status differences rarely cause problems because everyone shares a common ignorance (of the organisation).

Where the recruitment intake to the organisation is so low or irregular that a routine induction programme is unsuitable, it is useful to consider using a 'buddy' system whereby the new employee is paired up with a colleague who will help them through the induction process, arrange introductions and show them around the site etc, and be the prime person to be contacted for any help on where to find things etc, in the future. This is not simply a social nicety for the new employee; it is far more efficient in eliminating the potential for wasted time of the new employee 'exploring' useless avenues of information when a quick call could put them right. The 'buddy' system can either be a very informal arrangement or it can be formalised into the appointment of a number of suitable people trained to deliver all the aspects of induction. The careful selection of such people will also ensure that the perception of the company is conditioned by the people whom the organisation values. It is sad to realise that even in today's world of work, sub-cultures of subversive and sometimes malicious groups operate; such groups rarely turn down the opportunity to 'induct' new employees into 'their' working methods and outlook.

Competency-based induction

Some of the difficulties faced in planning induction are often reflections of the difficulties arising from the selection process itself. Where the specification or decision, or both, are unclear it is possible that candidates are recruited because they 'seem suitable' or are 'not particularly strong, but should be okay' or other vague reasons. While there may be concerns about the candidate not being wholly suitable for the role, it is not easy to articulate what those concerns are and therefore not easy to plan how they should be handled when the new person starts work. Equally, even where there are no such concerns, it is difficult, when appointing someone on generalisations of suitability, to be clear about individual strengths and weaknesses. The competency-based approach to selection ensures that the person-specification is broken down into its constituent parts, related to performance in the role, and expressed in clearly understandable terms and described in the behaviours one would expect to see in the workplace. The advantage, from an induction viewpoint, is that it is possible to be very specific about where the candidate does or does not match the specification. It then becomes easier to plan induction, development, and the everyday management of that person to play on the strengths and accommodate the weaknesses. Table 18 gives an extract from a competency-based report on a candidate, which provides very useful input into all these processes.

The profile of the candidate used for making the selection decision needs to be conveyed to the person responsible for managing them. This is likely to have been done as part of the selection decision, since good practice will have ensured that their manager is involved in such a decision, but there is a danger that once the decision is made the information may be neglected. It is important to highlight the applicability of the

Table 18
EXTRACT FROM A COMPETENCY-BASED REPORT

Achievement orientation

He has a much higher level of energy and drive than most people (achieving sten 9). People with his style are often perceived as very organised, disciplined and thorough. The strengths of his style are that he will readily accept responsibility and pursue his objectives energetically. He seems to have the motivation to try to make the most of what is done and get the best results (Belbin 'Shaper').

On the negative side, he may find it difficult to switch off from work. He may also find it difficult to accept people who don't have the same sense of purpose and career direction, or who have different values and standards.

Development advice

To increase his personal effectiveness, he should think about the following development points:

1. Establishing whether other people are committed to the task.
2. Considering other people's ideas and proposals and being prepared to negotiate and compromise.
3. Showing that he understands that other people may see things differently.
4. Finding ways of switching off from work.

profile to the work situation. This will enable the manager to plan for and manage the new person effectively. Thus, for example, if the profile indicates that the employee is very high on creativity and low on attention to detail, while the job specification asked for above-average creativity and average attention to detail, the decision may have been made that the candidate was sufficiently close to the profile to merit the selection. (The descriptions 'average' and 'below average' would not be used in practice, but are used here for illustration). While this decision may be the correct one for selection purposes, it needs to be realised that there will be implications for the way in which the role is fulfilled. It may, for example, be that the employee will be inclined to take risks, or not pay sufficient attention to the implementation details of new assignments, or may be weak in project planning (other elements of the candidate profile will contribute to the picture). It may be necessary to identify training programmes if these are appropriate (eg project management) or redesign the role (eg allocating implementation planning to another section) or paying particular attention to the potential risks in the day-to-day management or supervision of the employee.

Consideration needs to be given to whether the competencies are natural, acquired or adapting. Where the shortcomings are natural competencies (ie underlying personality characteristics) there will be little point in arranging training programmes since they will not be effective in making a change. In such cases, attention will need to be given to the way in which the individual is managed or to redesigning or restructuring the work to build in checks and balances. Where the shortfall occurs among acquired competencies (ie knowledge, experience, qualifications) it may be appropriate to plan training and development opportunities, assuming the shortfall is not unduly difficult or expensive to make good. For shortfalls in the adapting competencies (ie how the individual applies natural abilities and acquired skills) particular attention will need to be paid to the early stages of an induction programme to help the employee adapt to the new role or organisation, and consideration will need to be given to providing higher concentrations of management support, particularly during periods of change.

While 'general' induction can still be delivered through general induction programmes or buddy systems, the competency approach enables the remainder of the induction to be carefully tailored to the needs of the individual and focused on the most appropriate intervention, whether training, supervision, or role redesign, rather than relying on 'sheep dip' training applied indiscriminately in the hope of getting people up to speed.

Using information

All organisations need good information in order to operate effectively. Invariably, decisions on marketing strategy will be informed by research on customers and markets, decisions on investment will be informed by financial predictions and the utilisation forecasts, etc. The decisions on the organisation's human resource strategies are no different in requiring information for their formulation. The difficulty, however, is that many organisations do not use the information that is available to them. A great deal of information is collected during the selection process, and subsequently abandoned when the assignment has been completed. Organisations need to capture by-product information and key data during the selection process and make them available to appropriate people afterwards.

By-product information is all the intelligence on markets, competitors, developments, etc, which is 'down loaded' from candidates during the selection process. This is not to say that sensitive information disclosed in confidence, perhaps during the interview, should be abused, but rather that the vast range of other information freely given may be very useful to the organisation in seeing trends and developments and thereby keeping abreast of current business affairs. Similarly, information on types of people available or the kind of work being sought or not sought (including variations on working themes) is important to shape future decisions. There may be, for example, the opportunity to put on an extra part-time night shift, or a need to reconsider expansion plans if there are early signals of problems in the labour market. Similarly, early news of the likely closure of the factory down the road may have an adverse effect on services or products supplied to them or have the effect of releasing extra cash into the local economy to increase demand for products or service. By-product information is not essential; it is simply additional knowledge which may from time to time prove useful.

There are some key data which are often ignored beyond the selection process. In planning future work or organisation structure and resource requirements it is important to have the information on things such as skill levels, working time, flexibility, availability, etc. The assessment of future training needs and current training effectiveness requires information on the abilities and potential of employees. Decisions on pay structures need to take account of the motives, values, and expectations of employees if they are to be effective. Organisation development and culture change require an understanding of the psychology of the workforce. The work and the expense of gathering such information at the time the various initiatives are proposed may be so daunting or expensive or contentious that it is not gathered. It seems strange that often in these cases the raw data are wasting away in employee files or selection assignment folders, and are not funnelled into an aggregated information database which could prove an invaluable guide to the development of human resource policies and practices. Although computerised human resources information systems are in place in many organisations – and frequently the systems provide a bridge from 'candidate' to 'employee' and integrate selection with other HR details – the information seems to be used for administrative purposes rather than research intelligence. However simple the selection process in an organisation, it is likely to be the most in-depth look that the organisation will take into the employee's work record, domestic circumstances, aptitude and personality than at any other stage in his or her employment. It seems a great pity that such a potentially useful insight does not continue to play a meaningful role in planning the individual and collective management of that person.

16

MEASUREMENT AND

EVALUATION

Statistics

It is important to measure the success of the selection activity. At the simplest level this means following through to see that the new employee is able to fulfil the requirements of the role, etc. It is not unthinkable that the selection decision could have been wrong and that the individual is not suited to the role. This is the importance of probationary periods and proper induction which are covered in Chapter 15. It is also necessary to evaluate the success of the selection function itself. This means looking at the fairness and effectiveness of the selection activity. Fairness is concerned with ensuring that the process does not discriminate against protected groups, and it needs steps to be taken to monitor how such groups survive each stage or technique in the selection process, and ensuring that they are properly represented as a proportion of the workforce. Such monitoring requirements are covered in Chapter 4.

Assessing the effectiveness of the selection function, although important, is not a common practice and there is also a great deal of disagreement between researchers on appropriate measures of effectiveness. The basic premise is that the natural laws of distribution will apply to employees and candidates as much as they apply to anything else. Thus, taking a group of people and measuring them against some criterion such as height, weight or age etc, there will be a distribution pattern which equates to a bell-shaped curve. The proportions either side of the mid-point will be equal and most people will be nearer to the mid-point than the extremes. In statistical terms the bell shaped curve is known as the 'normal distribution curve', and the difference between the smallest and greatest measure is the range, which is divided into sections known as 'standard deviations' so that 68 per cent of people will be within one standard deviation either side of the mid-point, 95 per cent of people will be within two standard deviations either side, and virtually all (99.7 per cent) will be within three standard deviations either side. Figure 8 should make this clear. Put simply, if the adult male population of a city was weighed, and the average weight was 11 stone with a range from eight to 14 stone, we should expect to see 34 per cent of the people between 10 and 11 stone, and 34 per cent between 11 and 12 stone (ie 68 per cent will be within one standard deviation above or below the mean). Similarly, we can expect that 95 per cent of the male population will be within two standard deviations from the mean so we can say that 97.5 per cent of the population will not weigh more than 13 stone, since the two tails (for men weighing 8–9 stone and 12–13 stone) each contain 2.5 per cent of the population. Such statistical analysis is an important element of occupational psychology. If a set of weighing scales were to be regarded as an ability test and we subsequently weighed newcomers to the city to see whether they were lighter or heavier than the present population, we could say that any male greater than 12 stone was at the 85th percentile (68 per cent plus the 16 per cent in the < 10 stone tail on the left). In other words, he would weigh as much as or more than 85 per cent of the general adult male population of the city, which provides some meaningful comparison or benchmark for his weight. Using these principles in trying to select people, we are attempting to see how they would compare to the rest of the 'population'.

Utility analysis

One of the main arguments, in proposing that the effectiveness of selection techniques should be evaluated, is to say that by improving the techniques, selectors should be able

Figure 8
THE NORMAL DISTRIBUTION

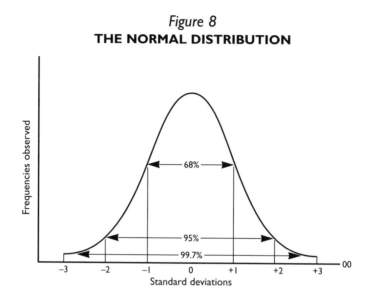

to select those who are at the higher levels of performance, ie those at the higher range of the bell-shaped curve. Thus, selectors ought to be looking to recruit those from the top 15 per cent of performance; put simply – trying to attract the best. Two problems emerge:

- What is the 'population'?
- How can all employers recruit 'the best'?

In looking at the population, should we be looking at a wide group of people or only at those suitable to undertake the role? Using these principles two researchers, Brogden and Hunter, developed a statistical method, called utility analysis, to assess the cost/benefit of improved selection procedures. The utility analysis is expressed as an equation thus:

$$(V \times Sr \times SDy \times 1 \times n) - (c \times n) = \text{£benefit}$$

In this equation V stands for the predictive validity of the particular technique or techniques used. This will range from 0 for no better than chance selection to 1 for perfect selection. For more information on validity see Chapter 7 on choosing techniques.

Sr stands for the selection ratio which, broadly speaking, is the proportion of people who would be suitable to fill the role. This is a tricky point since it does not relate to the whole population. Thus, for example, if we were looking to recruit brain surgeons we may say that the proportion of the population able to fill the role would be very small, but the selection ratio would be taken not from the population as a whole but those suitable to be considered, ie suitably qualified surgeons. The selection ratio would be those suitable to fill the role – a strange concept, given that all of them should be capable of filling the role. It will be derived by looking at how many were appointed from the candidate pool. Thus if 20 people applied and five were selected as suitable then the selection ratio would be 0.25 (one in four). One of the difficulties with this concept is that it assumes that those not selected are not suitable, but it may be the case that the number of suitable candidates outstripped the availability of positions. Although the figure of 0.25 was used to illustrate this example, it is not quite so simple to derive a selection ratio, and in the 1930s Taylor and Russell developed a set of statistical tables that have been universally applied.

SDy relates to the financial value of differences in performance. Thus, taking the normal distribution curve, what is the greater or lesser financial worth for a standard deviation above or below the mean? Put simply, how much better are the better performers than the poorer performers in financial terms to the organisation? In looking at a sales force, for example, it is possible to derive the normal distribution curve of performance by looking at sales generated (allowing for extraneous factors) and it is then possible to see how much more income is derived from the better performers. For service organisations and knowledge roles, this may not be so straightforward. Some researchers, in trying to quantify this, have quizzed managers and supervisors on the value of better performance and concluded, as a generalisation, that one standard deviation is equivalent to about 40 per cent of salary. This is partly attributable to research in the 1930s by Clark Hull which showed that, in skilled and semi-skilled jobs, the best performers achieved better productivity than the worse performers in a scale of ratios from 1.5: 1 to 2: 1.

l equals the length of service of the appointed people, *n* is the number of positions being filled, and *c* is the cost of the particular technique.

Thus, using a worked example for financial planning consultants, selling life insurance and related policies, it was decided to upgrade the selection system which consisted of an application form and interview, and change to a system which involved the application form, a structured interview, an ability test and a personality test. This would provide an improvement in predictive validity of 0.2. The selection ratio was 0.33, average length of service was about three years and 60 consultants were to be employed. The differences in income generated from various level of performers in the current population was analysed and determined to be £36,000. The additional cost of the improved selection method was £35 per person. The equation worked out at:

$$(0.2 \times 0.33 \times £36k \times 3 \times 60) - (£35 \times 60) = £426k$$

Researchers are particularly keen to improve techniques of utility analysis as a way of persuading practitioners to accept improved techniques for selection, and the associated additional cost. It is interesting to note, therefore, that it is not a widely used method for evaluating the effectiveness of the selection function. Recent research has shown that many line managers are not interested in the concept of the financial value of different performance levels. This may, at first, seem a strange finding and not wholly rational. Consider, nevertheless, the selection criteria for purchasing a car, where prospective purchasers:

- rate safety highly, while they regard the probability of an accident involving them as remote
- pay attention to the 0–60 acceleration and top speed, which the law will prevent them from using
- are very unlikely to take a test drive
- pay little regard to depreciation, running costs, and related aspects.

It may be unlikely that decisions on selection techniques are any more rational.

One of the interesting aspects of utility analysis is that it demonstrates that, where the proportion of candidates likely to succeed is fairly high, there is little point in investing in greatly improved selection techniques since their cost/benefit will be marginal.

Interesting though utility analysis may be, it is of limited use as a sales technique for persuading others to adopt improved practices, and it does not provide a refined basis for on-going evaluation of the effectiveness of the selection procedure used. It is, however, useful as a general guide in making decisions about the techniques to be used.

Measures

Given the difficulties of obtaining 'off the shelf' methods to assess the usefulness of techniques and the potential payback, it is important to develop measures internally which can be used as the quality control and pinpoint problems and opportunities. Measures should be looked at from the perspectives of:

- individual performance
- organisation performance.

The measures of individual performance may include such aspects as productivity (whether measured in output or sales or some similar measure), performance against quality criteria such as error rates, or level of competency, length of service in the organisation, or perhaps speed of promotion, and levels of absence. By gathering individual data on such measures, and comparing and contrasting with similar data for other employees, it is possible to discover whether the people recruited were a good choice, and therefore reflect on the quality of the selection process and decisions.

Organisation-wide measures can also be a useful indicator, particularly where there is a large proportion of recruitment intake which can influence the organisation on a dynamic basis. Such measures include productivity, quality measures such as error rates or downtime, absence rates, labour turnover, and measures of motivation and morale. The argument may be raised that these issues are too remote from decisions on selection to be a reflection of the quality of the selection process. The reality is, however, that they are all indicators of a potential mismatch between the people and the organisation, whether it be a mismatch with the role requirements or the organisation's aims. The purpose of selection is to ensure that there is a good match – which comes back to the comments on the normal distribution curve. The question has been posed,

> What happens if all employers try to improve their selection practices and aim to recruit the top 15 per cent?

The answer is, of course, that 'the top 15 per cent' is a myth; there are no 'best' people, simply the most suitable. This is the reason that selection cannot be regarded as a competition between candidates, or a competition with other employers to grab 'the best'. The primary role of recruitment and selection is to define the requirements that the organisation has for a certain kind of person, to go out and look for that kind of person, cause them to want to join the organisation, check that there is a match, bring the person into the organisation, and bring them up to speed at the earliest opportunity. Thus, measures of selection effectiveness cannot be external, they cannot be the product of academic research or other third-party views, they must be internal measures based on the organisation's aims and purpose.

REFERENCES AND

FURTHER READING

AKERLOF, G. A. (1970) 'The market for "a lemon" – quality uncertainty and the market mechanism'. *Quarterly Journal of Economics.* 84, 488–500.

ARGYRIS, C. (1962) *Interpersonal Competence and Organisational Effectiveness*. London, Tavistock Publishing.

ARGYRIS, C. (1971) *Management and Organisational Development: The path from XA to YB*. Maidenhead, McGraw-Hill.

BARRICK, M. *and* MOUNT M. (1991) 'The big five personality dimensions and job performance – meta-analysis'. *Personnel Psychology*. 44, 1–26.

BARTRAM D. (1997) 'Distance assessment – psychological assessment through the internet'. *Selection & Development Review*, Volume 13, No.2, 10–14.

BARTRAM, D., LINDLEY, P., MARSHALL, L. *and* FOSTER, J. (1995) 'Recruitment and selection of young people by small businesses'. *Journal of Occupational and Organisational Psychology*. 68, 339–358.

BELBIN, R. (1984) *Management Teams: Why they succeed or fail*. London, Heinemann.

BOAM, R. *and* SPARROW, P. (1993) *Designing and Achieving Competency*. Maidenhead, McGraw-Hill.

BOYATZIS, R. (1982) *The Competent Manager*. New York, John Wiley & Sons.

CAMPION, M., PURSELL, E. *and* BROWN, B. (1988) 'Structured interviewing – raising the psychometric properties of the employment interview'. *Personnel Psychology*. 41, 25–42.

CASCIO, W. *and* RAMOS, A. (1986) 'Development and application of a new method for assessing job performance in behavioural economic terms'. *Journal of Applied Psychology*. 71, 20–28.

COLLINSON, D. (1987) 'Who controls selection?'. *Personnel Management*. May.

COOK, M. (1991) *Personnel Selection and Productivity*. London, John Wiley & Sons.

COOPER, C. (1981) *Psychology and Management: A text for managers and trade unionists*. Leicester, The British Psychological Society.

DALESSIO, A. *and* SILVERHART, T. (1994) 'Combining biodata test and interview information – predicting decisions and performance criteria'. *Personnel Psychology*. 47, 303–315.

EYSENCK, H. T. (1947) *Dimensions of Personality*. London, Routledge.

FORSYTH, P. (1993) *Marketing for Non-Marketing Managers*. London, Institute of Management.

FOWLER, A. (1997) 'How to outsource personnel'. *People Management*. February.

FOX, S., BIZMAN, A., HOFFMAN, N. *and* OREN, L. 'The impact of variability in candidate profiles on rater confidence and judgement regarding stability and job situation'. *Journal of Occupational and Organisational Psychology*. 68, 13–23.

FURNHAM, A. *and* GUNTER, B. (1994) *Business Watching; Understanding Business Life*. London, ABRA Press.

FURNHAM, A., STEELE, H. *and* PENDLETON, D. (1993) 'A psychometric assessment of the Belbin team role self-perception inventory'. *Journal of Occupational Psychology*.

GRAVES, L. *and* POWELL, G. (1995) 'Effects of sex similarity on recruiters' evaluations of applicants'. *Personnel Psychology*. 48, 85–98.

GUNTER, B. *and* FURNHAM, A. (1993) *Consumer Profiles – an Introduction to Psychographics*. London, Routledge.

GUNTER, B., FURNHAM, A. *and* DRAKELY, R. (1993) *Biodata; Biographical Indicators of Business Performance*. London.

HERRIOT, P. *and* WINGROVE, J. (1984) 'Decision processes in graduate pre-selection'. *Journal of Occupational Psychology*. 57, 269–275.

HULL, C. L. (1920) 'Qualitative aspects of the evolution of concepts'. *Psychological Monographs* 123.

HULL, C. L. *Principles of Behavior*. New York, Appleton Century.

KLINE, P. (1995) 'Models and personality traits in occupational psychological testing'. *International Journal of Selection & Assessment*. Volume 3, no. 3, 186–190 July.

LATHAM, G. *and* WHYTE, G. (1994) 'The futility of utility analysis'. *Personnel Psychology*. 47, 31–46

LAWLER, E. (1981) *Pay and Organisation Development*. Reading, Mass., Addison Wesley.

MAEL, F., CONNERLEY, M. *and* MORATH, R. (1996) 'None of your business – parameters of biodata invasiveness'. *Personnel Psychology*. 49, 3, 613–650.

MCCLELLAND, D. (1961) *The Achieving Society*. Princeton, NJ, Van Nostrand.

MCCLELLAND, D. *and* BOYATZIS, R. (1982) 'Leadership motive pattern and long-term success in management'. *Journal of Applied Psychology*. 67, 737–43.

MCCRAE, R. *and* COSTA, P. (1989) 'More reasons to adopt the five-factor model'. *American Psychologist*. 44, 451–2.

MCDOUGALL, W. (1932) *The Energies of Man*. London, Methuen.

MCHENRY, R. (1997) 'Finding the norm for psychometric tests'. *People Management*, January.

MINTZBERG, H. (1994) *The Rise and Fall of Strategic Planning*. Hemel Hempstead, Prentice Hall.

PEARN, M. *and* KANDOLA, R. (1988) *Job Analysis*. London, Institute of Personnel Management.

PITT, G. (1995) *Employment Law*. 2nd edn, London, Sweet & Maxwell.

PLUMBLEY, P. (1974) *Recruitment & Selection*. 2nd edn, London, Institute of Personnel Management.

PULAKOS, E. *and* SCHMITT, N. (1995) 'Experience based and situational interview questions – studies of validity'. *Personnel Psychology*. 48, 289–308.

RANKIN, N. (ed.) (1997) 'The state of selection – developments in basic methods'. *Employee Development Bulletin*. 89, May.

ROBERTS, G. (1996) *Pay – Strategy Design & Negotiation*. Hertfordshire, Technical Communications Publishing.

SACKETT, T. *and* ROTH, L. (1996) 'Multi-stage selection strategies'. *Personnel Psychology*. 49, 3, 549–572.

SMITH, M. and ROBERTSON, I. (1991) *Advances in Selection and Assessment*. Manchester, John Wiley & Sons.

TAYLOR, H. C. and RUSSELL, J. T. (1939) 'The relationship of validity co-efficience to the practical effectiveness of tests in selection – discussion and tables'. *Journal of Applied Psychology*. 23, 565–578.

TERPESTRA, D. (1996) 'Recruitment and selection – the search for effective methods'. *HR Focus*. 16–17, May.

TETT, R., JACKSON, D. and ROTHSTEIN, M. (1991) 'Personality measures as predictors of job performance – a meta-analytic review'. *Personnel Psychology*. 44, 703–742.

TOPLIS, T., DULEWICZ, V. and FLETCHER, C. (1991) *Psychological Testing; A Manager's Guide*. 2nd edn, London, Institute of Personnel Management.

WALSH, J. (1996) 'Multinational management strategy and HR decision making in the single European market'. *Journal of Management Studies*. 33, 663–648.

WHINCUP, M. (1995) *Modern Employment Law; a Guide to Job Security and Safety*. Oxford, Butterworth Heinemann.

WOOD, R. (1997) 'The interview – just when you thought it was safe . . .'. *Selection & Development Review*. Volume 13, no.2, 15–17.

WOODRUFFE, C. (1990) *Assessment Centres*. London, Institute of Personnel Management.

INDEX